This book if borrowed
by a friend,
Right welcome
shall he be.
To read, to study
...not to lend,
But to return to me

Not that imparted
knowledge doth
Diminish learnings store
But books I find
if often lent,
Return to me
no more.

Gerald Slattery

ADVENTURES AND DISCOVERIES OF

Marco Polo

ADVENTURES AND
DISCOVERIES OF
MARCO POLO

BY RICHARD J. WALSH

Illustrated by CYRUS LEROY BALDRIDGE

RANDOM HOUSE · NEW YORK

SIXTH PRINTING

Copyright 1953 by Richard J. Walsh

All rights reserved under International and
Pan-American Copyright Conventions
Published in New York by Random House, Inc.
and simultaneously in Toronto, Canada by
Random House of Canada Ltd.
Library of Congress Catalog Card Number: 53–6270
Manufactured in the U.S.A

This book is based upon Marco Polo's own book. Not one bit of conversation or quotation has been invented by me. All quoted matter is taken from the well-known Marsden edition. Marco dictated his book in Italian. Since the translation into English was made about 100 years ago, when the English language was stiffer than it is now, I have sometimes used simpler words. But the sense is the same, and nothing has been added.

Some of the facts have been taken from other books.

R.J.W.

Contents

ADVENTURES AND DISCOVERIES OF

Marco Polo

1

A Boy of Venice

MARCO WAS seventeen years old when his great adventure began. He lived in Venice, the Italian city with canals for streets. His father, Nicolo Polo, and his uncle, Maffeo, were noblemen. Trading in jewels, silks and other valuable goods, they had once traveled far across Asia, even to China. There they had been received by the great Kublai Khan, ruler of most of Asia.

The Polos had been the first men of Europe ever to go to China. The Khan had asked them

many questions, which they were able to answer because on their long journey they had learned the Mongol language which he spoke. He had given them feasts and urged them to return.

Therefore in the year 1271 they set out again. This time they took the young Marco with them. So Marco became the first boy of the western world ever to see China.

He stayed for many years and came home with such tales of the wonders he had seen that people did not believe him. The book he wrote was not taken seriously so long as he lived. Because people thought he was exaggerating, they nicknamed him "Marco Millions." But he said calmly, "I have not told half of what I saw."

What he told had its influence upon the discovery of America. For Christopher Columbus read Marco's book. A copy of this book still exists today with notes in the handwriting of Columbus. Hoping to find a passage by the westward sea to the rich lands about which Marco had written, Columbus sailed across the Atlantic. He took with him a map made from Marco's descriptions. This map showed Japan and other islands as the first lands west of Europe. No one knew then that the continent of America lay between.

Later, Marco's account of the wealth of furs in Siberia led Henry Hudson to seek a northwest passage. In his search he explored the Hudson River and discovered Hudson Bay.

Two hundred years before Europe ever heard of America, a great deal was known about Asia, thanks to Marco. In time he came to be called "The Father of Geography."

2

Kublai Khan

THE THREE Polos stood before Kublai Khan in his magnificent court. Young Marco looked sturdy and tanned after the long journey across sea and rivers, mountains, plains and deserts. "And who is this?" asked the Khan when he saw Marco.

"That is your servant," said Nicolo, "and my son."

"He is welcome," said the Khan, "and it pleases me much." Turning to an officer, he gave the order that Marco be enrolled among his attendants of honor. Then he ordered that a great feast be prepared.

Afterward Marco described this and other feasts to show the splendor of Kublai Khan, which, he said, "is unequaled by that of any monarch on earth."

The walls of the great hall were decorated in gilt and silver and red lacquer with carved figures of dragons, birds, animals, warriors and pictures of battles. On the ceiling, said Marco, "nothing besides gilding and painting is to be seen." High up stood the throne. Before it was placed a table where the Khan was seated, with the empress on his left. Marco, describing the Khan, said, "he is neither tall nor short; his limbs are well formed and in his whole figure there is a just proportion. His complexion is fair, and occasionally suffused with red, like the bright tint of the rose, which adds much grace to his countenance. His eyes are black and handsome, his nose well shaped and prominent."

At a lower table were seated the Khan's twenty-two sons. The eldest was raised a little above the others whose heads were on a level with the Khan's feet. At still lower tables were the wives of the sons, the grandsons, the princes and the nobility, and then the military officers and their wives and the wives of the nobility, each placed according to rank. But not all who attended could be placed at tables; thousands sat on carpets, and thousands more stood outside the open doors. At each door stood two gigantic officers with staves in their hands. Their duty was to prevent anyone from touching the threshold, which was thought to be an evil omen.

Seated as he was, the Khan could overlook the entire hall. The many waiters who served him had their noses and mouths covered with handsome silk scarves, so that their breath might not fall upon his food. When he called for a drink, the page who brought it retired three paces and knelt, upon which all the guests also knelt. "At the same moment," Marco said, "all the musical instruments, of which there are many, begin to play, and continue until he has ceased drinking, when all the company rise again. This reverent salutation is made every time his majesty drinks." The music was played mostly by flutes, harps and lutes.

The quantity and richness of the food, and of the plate on which it was served, were incredible to Marco. Waiters constantly moved among the guests, asking if any wanted more meat or drink. When all had eaten their fill, the tables were taken away, and into the hall trooped clowns and musicians, tumblers and jugglers to show off their skill.

Another kind of feast was given on the Khan's birthday in September. On this day he wore a superb gown made of cloth of gold. Twenty thousand nobles and military officers wore gowns just like his, except that they were made of silk of the color of gold.

But the greatest feast of all was on the first of February, which in China was the beginning of the New Year. Everyone in all the countries subject to the Khan wore white on this day, as he did himself, because white was the emblem of good fortune. At the court the princes and the nobles of all ranks embraced one another, saying, "May good fortune attend you through the coming year," and Marco remarked, "as we ourselves are accustomed to do." They went about to one another's houses, exchanging gifts, always white ones.

From all his dominions came white gifts for the Khan. Chief among these were no less than one hundred thousand white horses. In making gifts

to the Khan it was the custom to give nine times nine of whatever was chosen, so that each province able to give white horses had to send eighty-one.

Five thousand elephants owned by the Khan marched in procession. Each was covered with cloth richly worked in gold and silk with figures of birds and animals. Then came a great train of camels. These, like the elephants, were laden with the gifts sent to the Khan. All passed in review before him, and after he had cast his eyes over the array of gifts, the tables were spread for the feast.

Again there were music and a show given by clowns and acrobats. While the Khan watched, a tiger was brought to him, so tame that it lay at his feet.

Such was the magnificence of the great Khan's court.

3

Tales of the Journey

Young Marco quickly felt himself at home in the Khan's court. He learned the ways and the language of the Mongols who were the rulers of China, which they had conquered long before. He soon found that the Khan liked to hear about far-away places and the customs of strange peoples. The Khan spent many hours listening to Marco's account of the long journey from Venice.

The Polos had crossed the Mediterranean Sea in a little sailing ship, landing at a port on the shore of Asia Minor. There they joined a caravan of merchants who traded in spices, drugs, silk, gold, jewels and ivory. They started into Armenia, where they learned that their journey was to be a dangerous one. The Sultan of Egypt had lately conquered most of Syria, and had already invaded Armenia, plundering and burning towns and killing or making captives of all Christians. The Polos were Christians, but, said Marco boldly, they were "undismayed by perils or difficulties" and they went on their way.

In the central part of Armenia they saw a high and wide mountain. On its summit was snow, which, they were told, never melted, but became deeper with each snowstorm. This was Mount Ararat. The people called it "the mountain of the ark," for they believed that it was here that Noah's Ark had come to rest.

It was here, too, that Marco heard about a remarkable place to the north. It was on the Caspian Sea. "There is a fountain of oil," said Marco, "with a flow so great that it supplies loads for many camels. It is not used for food, but as a salve for skin troubles in men and animals, and for other ills. It is also good for burning. In the country roundabout no other oil is used in the lamps, and people come from far away to get it." Here Marco was telling about what we now know as the famous oil fields of Baku, in southern Russia, where Joseph Stalin was born.

The Caspian was a vast lake. There were several islands in it, on which were fine castles. Some of these were the homes of families who had fled before the attacks of Kublai Khan's great ancestor, Genghis, who had laid waste all of Persia.

There were also traces of an earlier conqueror, Alexander the Great. From Persia he had tried to march northward into the Caucasus. But he was stopped at a narrow and difficult pass. On one side was the sea; on the other high mountains and forests. "A very few men," said Marco, "could defend it against the whole world." Since his own army could not get through, Alexander decided to fortify the pass so that the people north of it could not invade Persia. He built a great wall, with tow-

ers, so strong that it was called "The Gate of Iron."

But these were places to which Marco himself could not go. Instead they pressed straight on toward China.

Riding horseback or on donkeys, or sometimes in a jolting cart, the Polos traveled southeastward. By night they camped in tents at places where there was water, at oases, or on the banks of rivers or lakes. Sometimes they could board a river boat and travel downstream for a long distance.

Persia, they found, was "anciently a large and

noble country, but now in large part destroyed by the Mongols." Coming to a place called Saveh, Marco learned that it was from here that the Three Wise Men had come to adore the Christ Child in Bethlehem. Their names were Baldasar, Gaspar and Melchior. They were buried together in Saveh, "in a fair sepulcher, and they were all three entire with their beards and hair." Marco asked many people about them, but nobody could tell him anything except that they had been buried "in ancient times."

Three days' journey from there brought Marco to a castle of fire-worshipers. Here the fire-worshipers told him that long ago three kings of their country had gone to adore a certain king who was newly born. They had taken with them gold, frankincense and myrrh. The infant king had given them a closed box. After carrying the box for several days, they opened it and found a stone in it. They were surprised and threw it in a pit. Instantly fire burst forth. When they saw this, they repented what they had done, and taking up some of the fire, carried it home. Ever since they had kept the fire burning and adored it as a god. The fire in the pit into which they had thrown the stone had never gone out. "That is why the people of that country worship fire," said Marco.

At length the Polos came to Hormuz, on an island at the base of the Persian Gulf. Hormuz was a port visited by traders from all parts of India, who brought spices and drugs, precious stones, pearls, gold tissues, ivory and other goods.

It was summer. Every day from about nine o'clock to noon, a land wind blew, so hot that one could hardly breathe, and many died of suffocation. During this season everyone went over to the mainland and took refuge in shaded gardens. While Marco was there, he had grim proof of the effect of this extreme heat. The ruler of Hormuz had failed to pay his annual tribute to the king of Kerman in Persia. The king of Kerman therefore sent an army of 1,600 horsemen and 5,000 foot soldiers to attack the people while they were on the mainland. But the army was misled by its guides and, overtaken in the open by the hot wind, died to the last man.

The Polos had intended to take a ship at Hormuz and sail for China. But, said Marco, "we found that the vessels built at Hormuz are of the worst kind, and dangerous for navigation." The wood used in them was so hard that nails could not be driven into it. Wooden pins were driven into holes bored at stem and stern. "After this," said Marco, "they are bound together with a kind of rope-yarn, stripped from the husks of cocoanuts. Pitch is not used for preserving the bottoms of the vessels, but they are smeared with an oil made from the fat of fish, and then caulked with oakum. The vessel has no more than one mast and one deck. When she has taken in her cargo, it is covered over with hides, and upon these hides they place the horses which they carry to India. They have no iron anchors, but instead use another kind of ground-tackle. The result is that in bad weather —and these seas are very stormy—they are often driven on shore and lost."

After seeing how poor the ships were, the

Polos turned northward, retracing their steps and planning to go all the way to China overland.

Their first hardship was crossing the terrible salt desert of Kerman. At the plodding pace of the caravan of camels, horses and donkeys, it took seven days to cross this desert. "For the first three days," said Marco, "little water is to be found and that little is full of salt and green as grass, and so nauseous that no one can drink it." They forded a river of liquid salt which came up to their horses' knees. On both sides of the river the desert was covered with a crust of white salt, like frozen snow, which crackled under the horses' hoofs. The men carried with them a supply of drinking water, but the animals, driven by thirst, drank from the river and became sick. The whole region was arid and desolate. For three days not one building was seen, and no animals because there was nothing for them to eat.

On the fourth day they came to a river of fresh water. Its channel was mostly underground, but here and there the force of the current had broken through the surface and there was plenty of wa-

Route of Marco Polo from 1272 to 1294

0 MILES 500

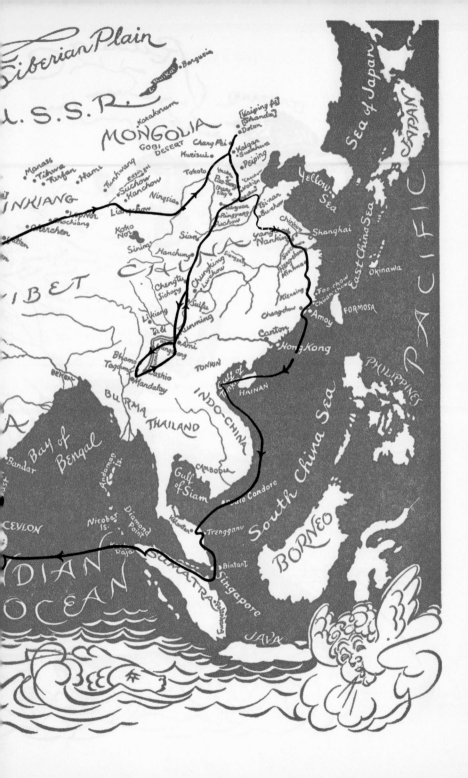

ter for man and beast. The weary travelers paused to rest for a while before starting on another three days of struggle with the desert.

This was by no means their last desert. But now, traveling northeastward, they came often to fine, fertile plains, with busy market places in the fortified cities, and great castles on the hills.

They crossed a wide plain where, the people told Marco, a great battle had been fought between Alexander, King of Macedonia, and Darius, the Persian. But more remarkable, in Marco's eager eyes, was a dry and fruitless tree, called "the tree of the sun," or *arbor secco*. Marco carefully kept a description, "It is tall with a large trunk. Its leaves are green on the upper side, but white on the under. It produces husks like those in which the chestnut is enclosed, but these contain no fruit. The wood is solid and strong, and yellow in color. There is no other species of tree near it for a hundred miles, except in one direction where trees are found within about ten miles."

They left Persia and moved on into what is now Afghanistan. Here they passed through a town which produced "the best melons in the world," as Marco said, "sweet as honey."

Next the Polos came to Balkh, a large and magnificent city which has since been called "the mother of cities." Here again Marco saw the effects of the invasion made by the Mongols who had swarmed from the East under Genghis Khan, the mighty ancestor of the Khan whom they were to visit. Marco said, "It contained many palaces built of marble, and spacious squares, still visible, although in ruins. It was in this city, according to the report of the inhabitants, that Alexander took to wife the daughter of King Darius."

Marco was making notes about many kinds of animals and birds and fish. At Kishm he discovered porcupines, and very likely it was the description he gave of them that started the story that many people still believe. "They roll themselves up," he said, "when the hunters set their dogs at them, and with great fury shoot out the quills or spines with which their skins are furnished, wounding both men and dogs."

One of Marco's discoveries on this long journey

was indeed historic. As it left the plains, the caravan began to climb northeastward. Ascending
"mountain after mountain," Marco said, "you at
last reach a point of the road where you might sup-
pose the surrounding summits to be the highest
lands in the world. Here, between two ranges you
see a large lake, from which flows a handsome river along an extensive plain covered with
the richest verdure. The leanest cattle turned upon
it become fat in ten days. For twelve days the trail
is along this high plain, which is called Pamir."
Thus Marco became the first person from the outside world to mention and describe The Pamirs,
famous today among travelers and geographers.

"The mountains are so high that no birds are
to be seen near their summits," and he reported
that fires do not give the same heat or cook food so
well as at lower altitudes. To the sea-faring Venetians and to the Khan, who lived close to sea
level, this was wonder indeed.

On The Pamirs Marco made one of his unique
discoveries. "In this plain," he said, "there are a
great many wild animals, particularly sheep of a

large size, having very large horns. Of these horns the shepherds make ladles and vessels for holding their food, and build fences of horns for enclosing their cattle and protecting them against the wolves. The horns and bones of the sheep are found in great quantities. Heaps are made of them at the sides of the road to guide travelers at the season when it is covered with snow."

His story of these big-horn sheep was so vivid, and so new to Europe, that the experts who classify animals later gave to them the Latin name, *ovis poli*, or Polo's sheep. And famous hunters have gone on expeditions to The Pamirs to find these great sheep with curved horns which Marco was the first to describe.

4

The Great Desert

THEY WERE twelve days on the great plateau of The Pamirs and then climbed on toward the northeast.

"We went over mountains and through valleys in constant succession," said Marco, "and passed many rivers and desert tracts. In the highest of these mountains there lives a tribe of savage, ill-disposed and idolatrous people, who feed on the animals they can destroy and clothe themselves with their skins."

After forty more days they reached Kashgar, which in Chinese is called Shufu. For here they first entered a region which is part of China, in the province of Sinkiang. Marco had to begin to learn a new language.

Kashgar was a great trading center, into which came caravans from east, west, north and south, and from which merchants went out to all parts of the known world. It was a place of fine gardens, orchards and vineyards, and of wide fields of cotton, flax and hemp. "But in truth," said Marco, "they are a greedy, sordid race, eating badly and drinking worse."

Kublai Khan could not be much offended by

Marco's low opinion of the people of Kashgar. For although they were his subjects, they were not truly either Chinese or Mongols. They had formerly been an independent kingdom and had been conquered by his ancestor, Genghis. They were ruled now by one of the younger relatives of the Khan named Kaidu, of whom Marco was to hear more later.

On and on went the travelers—five days through the province of Kashgar, five days to Soche, eight days to Hotien, five days to Yutien, ten days to Lop. Marco was careful to remark that each of these places was under the rule of the great Khan.

At Lop they stood on the edge of a vast desert. Here they must halt for a long time, to rest from the fatigue of their travel over mountains and plains, and to prepare for their mastery of the widest desert of all. It would take a month to cross the narrowest part. To travel its length would be impossible, because that would take a year, and food and supplies for so long a time could not be carried. They packed their food on donkeys and camels. When a donkey's load was gone, he was to be killed and eaten. The camels could hold out longer, because they carried larger loads and needed less food for themselves.

The Polos set out at last on the desert. For a whole month they traveled over sandy plains or barren mountains. But the road was so well planned that, as Marco said, "at the end of each day's march you stop at a place where there is water—not enough for large numbers, but enough for a hundred persons, and their animals. At three or four of these halting places the water is salt and bitter, but at the others, about twenty, it is sweet and good. Neither beasts nor birds are seen, because there is no kind of food for them."

In the desert Marco heard some strange stories. Older men told him that the desert was "the abode of many evil spirits." Persons who dropped behind their caravan, perhaps falling asleep until the caravan was out of sight over a hill, would hear themselves called by name, even in the familiar voice of one of their companions. Following the voice, they would be led away from the road and would be lost and die in the desert. At night, sometimes, they would hear the march of a caravan on the road, and following it in the dark, would be led astray to die. Sometimes the spirits would even look like their traveling companions. Sometimes what seemed a body of armed men would ride toward them, driving them to flight across the desert, and to death from hunger. The air would be filled with the sound of drums, with the music of many instruments, the clash of arms.

Such tales Marco repeated, although he did not say that any of these things had happened to him. People dismissed them as "idle stories." But later explorers found that in that desert there are indeed various strange noises. These are caused by the constant shifting, in the heat of the sun or the cool of the night, of the myriads of particles of sand, and these are in themselves like musical instruments and could make sounds like human voices. The rest is imagination or superstition.

5

Siberia and the Mongols

CROSSING THE DESERT on the old well-marked caravan road from Persia, Marco was far south of the trail which his father and uncle had followed on their first trip to China. They had then gone into Russia and had come down into China by the northern route through Samarkand and Urumchi and Hami.

Marco was going to miss seeing Russia. But he was told much about it by his elders on the long trek, and by other travelers whom he met. Russia, he learned, was a vast land. Like China, much of it had been conquered by the Mongol khans or paid tribute to them. The Mongol Prince Sain had led the invasion of Europe more than thirty years before. His rule and that of his successors reached as far west as the Caucasus, Crimea and the Danube River.

In the north of Russia there was the Region of Darkness, which we now call Siberia, where during most of the winter the sun was never seen. The light was just about what we have at dawn, Marco said, "when we may be said to see and not to see. Russia is a very cold region and I have been assured that it extends even as far as the Northern Ocean." The people were tall, handsome and of fair complexion, but they were "brutalized, dull and stupid."

South and west of Siberia were the Mongols. They often raided and plundered Siberia in the months of darkness. The Mongols had a trick for finding their direction in the dark. They would ride into Siberia on mares whose young foals were left behind. When the raid was over, the riders dropped the reins and the mares carried them straight back to where the foals were.

The Mongols themselves were nomads. They did not like to live in towns or castles. They were always in the open plains or valleys or mountains, according to the changing seasons. They did not plant crops, but lived on the meat and milk of the vast herds of horses, cows and sheep that they drove as they moved from place to place. They drank the milk of mares as well as that of cows.

In ancient times, according to legend, the Mongol tribes had been oppressed by a powerful prince, and had migrated northward across the Gobi Desert. They had built a strong earthen wall at Karakorum. About 1187 they had chosen Genghis Khan as their ruler, who soon began to dream of conquering the whole world.

At the time each town or district was governed by the people themselves, or by a petty king. One by one these fell before the attacks of the Mongols.

After many years of victories, Genghis Khan was at last struck down in battle by an arrow. He died of the wound. Sons and grandsons succeeded to the title of Khan, which meant emperor. Kublai Khan was sixth of the line.

The roving masses of Mongols carried with them round tents made of felt. They had two-wheeled carts drawn by camels or oxen in which the women and children rode. The women prepared food for the family and did the trading. The men spent their time in hunting and training for war. From early childhood boys were taught to use the bow and arrow. They learned to stay on horseback for as long as two days and nights, sleeping in the saddle while their horses grazed.

When one of the Mongol chiefs went on a war-like expedition, he put himself at the head of one hundred thousand horsemen. Each man had eighteen horses with him. Sometimes when they had to move fast and could not stop to prepare food, they would open veins in their horses and drink the blood.

It was those Mongols still living north of the desert who robbed the Siberian people. This was profitable because the Siberians had a wealth of

furs. During the summer they had almost constant daylight. They used it to catch vast quantities of fur-bearing animals—ermines, martens, sables, foxes.

Among the northern Mongols there was also a crude tribe of men who rode on reindeer, and ate their meat. The flat country to the south was partly desert and partly swamp. Most of the year it was frozen over. For travel these tribesmen used sleds drawn by six strong dogs. There were stages

35

where the dog teams could be changed and the travelers could spend the night. Thus the valuable furs were sent out for sale in the other parts of Russia and in Europe, and to the Khan in China.

Marco heard a great deal about the fighting that went on between the Mongols themselves. Nephews and other relatives of Kublai Khan were forever getting into fights. One of them, Kaidu, the ruler in Turkestan, had actually started a great war against the Khan. There were many fierce battles. In one of them, Marco was told, they "fought like mortal enemies." The field was "covered with so many corpses that it was pity to see, and many a woman that day was made a widow, and many a child an orphan." In that battle Kaidu was so badly beaten that he had to retreat all the way to Samarkand.

This King Kaidu had a daughter named Shining Moon. She was so tall and strong and well-built that she was almost a giant. She could wrestle with any young man in the kingdom and beat him. Her father wanted her to marry. But she said that she would not marry any man who could not overcome her by force. Her father then gave her a written promise that she could marry of her own will. This was proclaimed all over the known world. Men came from everywhere. Any who could throw her could have her as wife. Any who lost must forfeit to her a hundred horses. Before long she had more than ten thousand horses.

At last, as in all such legends, there came a young and handsome prince, son of a powerful king. He brought with him a thousand beautiful horses. King Kaidu very much wanted this rich youth as his son-in-law. He privately asked his daughter to let herself be beaten this time. She said she would not do so for anything in the world.

In the great hall the audience gathered, the king and queen sitting above them. In the rules of the contest it was decided that because the young prince was of such high rank he should forfeit the whole of his thousand horses if he was beaten. The king and the queen, and in fact everyone in the hall, wanted the prince to win. But Shining Moon threw him, and he lost his thousand horses!

Let us conclude the story in Marco's own

words: "After this the king took his daughter with him into many battles, and there was not a cavalier in the host who showed so much valor. And at last the damsel rushed into the midst of the enemy, and seizing upon a horseman, carried him off." To marry him, perhaps?

6

The Real China

AFTER THE thirty days' crossing of the great desert the Polos were at last in the real China. The first city was Tunhwang, in the province of Kansu. This was a place where the caravan roads met and to which pilgrims came from far and wide. For near here were the "Caves of a Thousand Buddhas." The multitude of idols of wood, stone and clay, covered with gilt, some small, some very large, some lying full length, some standing, made a deep impression on Marco's Christian mind.

The ways of the Chinese people immediately had a fascination for him. He told at length of marriage customs, and especially of the funerals, which were held only after astrologers had consulted the horoscope of the person who had died. He said, "The astrologers tell the relatives that the body must not be taken from the house through the principal door, because they have discovered from the aspect of the heavens, or otherwise, that this would be unlucky. It must be taken out from a different side of the house. Sometimes they require the family to break through the wall."

He noticed another funeral custom, which is still seen in modern China nearly 700 years later. He said, "They provide a number of pieces of paper, made of the bark of a certain tree, upon which are painted the figures of men, women, horses, camels, pieces of money, and dresses. These they burn along with the body, in the belief that in the next world the deceased will enjoy the services and use of the servants, cattle, and all the articles pictured on the paper. During the whole of the funeral all the musical instruments they possess sound with an incessant din."

Ten days after leaving their first Chinese city, the Polos came to Soochow. This is at the western end of the Great Wall of China, but at that point there was only a rampart of earth.

The next city was the chief one in the province, Kanchow, "large and magnificent." Marco found that here, while most of the people were idol-worshipers, there were also Moslems and some Christians. The Polos stopped here for a long time.

South of them lay the great lake Koko-Nor. In this region Marco observed a wild animal which, he said, "in point of size may be compared to elephants. Their color is a mixture of white and black, and they are very beautiful." Their hair was smooth except on the shoulders where it stood up high. This animal was the yak. Marco admired the hair, which was white and more soft and delicate than silk. He collected some of it to take home to Venice, where it was much admired. He also took home the head and feet of another handsome animal, something like a small antelope, which produced "the finest musk that is known." And he saw many birds with beautiful plumage, including huge pheasants.

At last the Polos found themselves on the great road that led from Tibet to the Khan's capital. As they rode northeast, they began to see plainly the signs of the mighty power and wide influence of the Khan.

About every twenty-five or thirty miles they came to a "post-house," a large handsome building with well-furnished rooms, hung with silk and supplied with everything that a weary traveler could want. "Fit for princes," said Marco. "At each of these post-houses four hundred good horses were kept in constant readiness, in order that all messengers going and coming upon the business of the grand Khan, and all ambassadors, may have relays, and, leaving their jaded horses, be supplied with fresh ones. Ambassadors to the court, and the royal messengers, go and return through every province and kingdom of the empire with the greatest convenience and speed. In all of this the grand Khan shows his superiority over every other emperor, king, or human being. In his dominions no less than two hundred thousand horses are thus used, and ten thousand buildings, with suitable furniture, are kept up. It is indeed so wonderful a system and so effective in its operation, as it is scarcely possible to describe."

Between the post-houses were small villages, about three miles apart. "In these are stationed the foot-messengers, who are also employed in the service of the Khan. They wear girdles around their waists, to which several small bells are attached, in order that their coming may be heard at a distance. As they run only three miles from one of these foot-stations to the next one, the bells give notice of their approach, and a fresh courier prepares to go on with the packet instantly upon its arrival. Thus it is so rapidly carried from station to station that in two days and two nights the Khan receives news from a distance that in the ordinary way could not come in less than ten days. It often happens that in the fruit season, what is gathered in the morning at Peking is brought to the Khan at Xanadu by the next evening, although the distance is usually counted as ten days' journey.

"At each of these three-mile stations there is a clerk, whose business is to make note of the day and hour at which one courier arrives and the other departs. This is likewise done at all the post-houses. Besides this, officers pay monthly visits to every station, in order to look into the management of them. Where it happens that there is a river or a lake which the foot couriers or the horsemen must cross, the neighboring cities are required to keep three or four boats in constant readiness."

Marco was astonished to learn of the speed of the Khan's mounted messengers. Their system was like that which became famous in America, six hundred years later, as the "Pony Express." Marco told of it as follows: "When it is necessary that the messengers should travel with extraordinary speed, as in the cases of bringing news of disturbance in any part of the country, the rebellion of a chief, or some other important matter, they ride two hundred or sometimes two hundred and fifty miles in the course of a day. They are mounted upon good fleet horses. They gird their bodies tight and bind a cloth round their heads. They push their horses to the greatest speed until they come to the next post-house, twenty-five miles away, where they find other horses, fresh and ready to go. They spring upon them without taking any rest. Changing in the same way at every stage until the end of the day, they can cover two hundred and fifty miles. In cases of great emergency they keep on their course during the night, and if there should be no moon, they are accompanied to the next station by persons on foot, who run before them with lights."

As the Polos went on, they found the great road lined with trees. Marco said, "There is another rule of the Khan that is equally ornamental and useful. At both sides of the public roads he causes trees to be planted, of a kind that become large and tall. Being only two paces apart, they serve (besides the advantage of their shade in summer) to point out the road when the ground is covered with snow. This is of great help and comfort to travelers. This is done along all the high roads, where the soil permits planting. When the road lies through sandy deserts or over rocky mountains, where it is impossible to have trees, the Khan orders stones to be placed or columns erected as guiding marks. He also appoints officers whose duty it is to see that all these are properly arranged and the roads constantly kept in good order."

With all this wonderful organization, it was not strange that the Khan heard of the approach of the travelers when they were still far away. They were forty days' journey from his court when they were met by messengers sent out by him. He had given orders that at every place through which they were to pass everything necessary for their comfort was to be done. Thus they were led in safety and honor to him.

When they arrived, the Khan was at his summer palace, north of Peking, at Xanadu.

The palace was built of marble and other

handsome stone. From each end of it, ran a wall sixteen miles in circuit, enclosing a royal park to which there was no entrance except through the palace. Many small streams flowed through the rich meadows in this park. At the center there was a beautiful grove of trees, in which stood a great pavilion, supported by a colonnade of pillars, gilt and varnished. Round each pillar was entwined the tail of a gilt dragon. The heads of the dragons held up the roof and their claws stretched right and left along the eaves. The roof was of split bamboo, also gilt, and the building was braced on every side, like a tent, by two hundred strong cords of silk. The whole was so cleverly built that it could be taken down like a modern circus tent and set up anywhere at the Khan's pleasure.

Marco soon learned that one of the Khan's favorite sports was falconry. He had in cages in the park more than two hundred hawks and other birds of the chase which he went to inspect at least once a week. Many deer and goats were pastured as food for the birds. "Often," said Marco, "when he rides about this enclosed forest, he has small leopards carried on horseback behind their keepers. When he pleases to give the order for them to be released, they instantly seize a stag or goat, or fallow deer, which he gives to his hawks. In this manner he amuses himself."

7

More Discoveries

Now a favorite at the court, Marco not only told the Khan of the discoveries he had made on his long journey, but also began to make new ones.

He was very much struck by the use of paper money, which at that time had never been heard of in Europe. He said jokingly that the Khan "may truly be said to possess the secret of the alchemists, because he has the art of producing money." Marco made notes of how paper bills

49

"*The splendor of Kublai Khan,*" *said Marco Polo,*

"is unequaled by any monarch on earth."

were made from the bark of mulberry trees, signed by the officials and stamped in vermilion with the royal seal. He said, "This paper currency is circulated in every part of the Khan's dominions, and no person, at the peril of his life, dares to refuse to accept it in payment. All his armies are paid with this currency, which to them is of the same value as if it were gold or silver. It may certainly be said that the Khan has a greater command of treasure than any other ruler in the universe."

A few Europeans had heard of coal at that time but not the people of Venice. What Marco told them when he got home was this: "In one province there is found a sort of black stone, which they dig out of the mountains, where it runs in veins. When lighted, it burns like charcoal, and retains the fire much better than wood, so that the fire can be kept during the night, and in the morning will be found still burning. These stones do not flame, except a little when first lighted, but they give out a considerable heat."

This seemed all the more important to Marco,

because he had never seen people who needed so much warm water as the Chinese. Their daily baths were a surprise to him. At home in Venice nobody bathed very much. So he wrote, "It is true that there is no scarcity of wood in the country, but the multitude of inhabitants is so immense, and their stoves and baths, which they are continually heating, so numerous, that wood could not supply the demand. For there is no person who does not take a warm bath at least three times in the week, and during the winter daily if possible. Every man of rank or wealth has a bath in his house for his own use. The stock of wood must soon prove too little for such consumption; while these black stones may be had in great abundance at a cheap rate."

Some believe that another Chinese invention which Marco took back was macaroni, for which Italy has become famous. At any rate, his book makes special mention of macaroni as a Chinese food. But it is a strange fact that he never even mentioned the chopsticks with which the Chinese eat, or the tea they drink in such quantities.

Marco was very much entertained by the Chinese magicians, as we still are today. He described one of their tricks: "So expert are they in their infernal art, they may be said to perform whatever they will. One example shall be given, although it may be thought to exceed the bounds of belief. When the Khan sits at meals in his hall of state, the table which is placed in the center is elevated and at a distance from it stands a large buffet, where all the drinking vessels are arranged. Now, by means of their supernatural art, the magicians cause the flagons of wine, milk or any other beverage, to fill the cups spontaneously, without being touched by the attendants, and the cups to move through the air the distance of ten paces, until they reach the hand of the Khan. As he empties them, they return to the place from whence they came; and this is done in the presence of such persons as are invited by his majesty to watch the performance."

Actually, Marco thought that this was not a trick, but something done by the "black magic" or supernatural power in which the people of his time firmly believed.

At one time the Khan himself, when the elder Polos asked him why he did not become a Christian, said to them that Christians could not do what his people could do. He went on, "When I sit at table, the cups that were in the middle of the hall come to me filled with wine or other drink, without being touched by human hand, and I drink from them." No doubt the trick was done with wires, invisible to the guests, and no doubt the Khan himself knew all about the wires.

But the Khan added in praise of his magicians, "They have the power of controlling bad weather and forcing it to retire to any quarter of the heavens, with many other wonderful gifts of that kind. You have seen that their idols have the faculty of speech, and predict to them whatever is required."

8

The Imperial City

WONDERFUL as Xanadu was, in December Marco went with the Khan to a place still more wonderful. This was the great city which was the capital of the Khan's entire empire, and where he spent the winter months.

Approaching the capital from the north, Marco began to see large towns, each surrounded by a high wall. These, he learned, lived mostly by manufacturing goods wanted by the Khan and his court. Further on, he passed into crowded suburbs, where merchants and others coming to do business with the court had handsome houses. "For," said Marco, "to this city everything that is most rare and valuable in all parts of the world finds its way. More especially this applies to India, which sends precious stones, pearls, and various drugs and spices. The quantity of goods sold there exceeds that of any other place. Every day no less than a thousand carriages and pack-horses, loaded with raw silk, make their entry. Gold tissues and silks of various kinds are manufactured to an immense extent. In the suburbs, as far perhaps as a mile from the city, there are at intervals many hotels, or caravanserais, in which live the merchants arriving from various places. To each description of people a separate building is assigned, as we should say, one to the Lombards, another to the Germans, and a third to the French." But here there were no French or Germans or other Europeans except the three Italians, Marco and his father and uncle.

After crossing a river, they came to a great gate set in a thick earthen wall which stretched for three miles on either side. Above the gate stood a handsome white structure. This was the guard-house. For the gate was guarded by a thousand soldiers.

Stopping to climb to the top of the wall, Marco saw another guardhouse exactly opposite on the other side of the city, six miles away.

Since what Marco now looked upon was the famous city which we know as Peking, let us read at some length his description of what he saw. Looking right and left, he saw that the city was square, six miles on each side, with three gates in each wall, and above each gate a guard-house. So the city had 12,000 soldiers to guard it! But, Marco, said, "It is not to be thought that such a force is stationed there because of fear of danger from any hostile power, but as a guard suit-able to the honor and dignity of the ruler."

The streets were perfectly straight, running from wall to wall, so that the whole city was laid out in squares like a checkerboard. In the center stood a tower in which hung a great bell. Marco learned that this bell sounded curfew every night.

After its third peal no one was allowed on the street except on urgent business, and then must carry a light. In daylight the streets were thronged with people coming and going, and were lined with shops and booths of every kind, gaily decorated with colored paint and gilt.

On the southern side of the city there was the rainbow gleam of many roofs of red, green, blue and violet tiles. For there stood the vast palace of the Khan, surrounded by squares of walls within walls. Along each side of the outer wall ran a deep moat. Inside was an open space where more soldiers were stationed. The inner wall had three gates on the north and three on the south. Each middle gate was a large one, and was opened only when the Khan passed through. Those on each side always remained open for ordinary traffic. In the middle of each division of the walls was a large, handsome building. There were in all eight of these buildings, in which the royal military equipment was kept—one building for each kind. Thus, the bridles, saddles, stirrups, and other cavalry equipment occupied one storehouse. The bows, strings, quivers, arrows, and other articles used in archery filled another; cuirasses, corselets, and other leather armor a third storehouse, and so on.

Within the walls also were lovely groves of trees, and rich green pastures in which were kept various kinds of animals, such as stags, roebucks and fallow deer. The roads across the pastures were raised three feet above their level, and paved so that no rain water or mud could collect upon them.

Finally, within the innermost wall, which was one mile square, twenty-five feet high and very thick, stood the palace of the Khan. "The largest palace that has ever yet been known," said Marco in wonder. Later he visited the palace, and this is his own description: "It reaches from the north to the south wall, leaving only a vacant court where persons of rank and the military guards pass and repass. It has no upper floor, but the roof is very high. The paved foundation on which it stands is raised above the level of the ground, and a wall of marble is built on all sides and serves as a terrace, where those who walk on it can be seen from outside. Along the outer edge of the wall is a handsome balustrade, with pillars, which the people are allowed to approach. The sides of the great halls and the apartments are ornamented with dragons in carved work and gilt, figures of warriors, of birds, and of beasts, with paintings of battle scenes. On each of the four sides there is a grand flight of marble steps, by which you ascend from the level of the ground to the terrace which is the approach to the palace itself. In the rear of the palace there are large buildings containing several rooms, where the private property of the monarch is kept, his treasure in gold and silver, precious stones and pearls, and his vessels of gold and silver plate. On the other side, opposite to the palace in which the emperor lives, is another palace, in every respect similar, the residence of his eldest son.

"On the northern side, about a bow-shot distance from the surrounding wall, is an artificial mountain of earth, the height of which is full a hundred paces, and the circuit at the base about a

On the artificial mountain is a pavilion of great beauty.

mile. It is covered with the most beautiful ever-green trees. Whenever his majesty hears of a handsome tree growing in any place, he has it dug up, with all its roots and the earth about them, and however large and heavy it may be, he has it transported by means of elephants to this mountain, and adds it to the collection. Because of this perpetual verdure it is called the Green Mountain. On its summit is an ornamental pavilion, which is also entirely green. The view of this altogether—the mountain itself, the trees, and the buildings—forms a delightful and wonderful scene."

9

Rebellion

THE CITY which Marco had seen and described was a new one, called Taidu. In modern Peking it is called the Tartar City, and the palace is called the Forbidden City. The ancient and once magnificent royal city of Canbalu lay close by on the other side of a small river.

The Khan had built Taidu in recent years because he had been warned that there were signs in Canbalu that the Chinese people were going to rebel against their Mongol ruler.

The warning had come from his astrologers, of

whom there were five thousand. The Khan supported these astrologers so that they could spend their whole time at their mysterious arts. They were the makers of almanacs. They had astrolabes with which through the whole year they studied the sky and the movements of the planets and the distant stars. They were the weathermen. They foretold each month whether there would be rain or thunderstorms. Sometimes they even predicted earthquakes.

They would also prophesy disasters, such as plagues, wars or conspiracies. They wrote out their predictions for the year and sold them for a small price to anyone who wanted to peer into the future. Anyone who was planning to take a long journey on business or to start some important work would go to an astrologer to learn what success he might be likely to have. The astrologer would ask him the year, the month, and the hour of his birth. Then he would look into the records and see what stars were in the ascendant at that time. Upon this would he base his prediction of success or failure.

Some years earlier these astrologers had warned the Khan that the city of Canbalu was destined to start a rebellion.

This seemed strange to Marco, because he thought that the Khan was a most kindly ruler, who tried to help the people. Every year he sent out men to see whether any of his subjects had had poor crops because of bad weather, or locusts or other pests. Wherever this had happened he excused them from paying the usual taxes or tribute that year. He also sold them from his own granaries, at one-fourth the usual price, as much grain as they needed for food, and seed for sowing their land. In times of good crops he bought large amounts of grain and stored it in granaries which were always kept full in order to provide for times of scarcity.

Breeders of cattle and sheep paid him as annual tribute one-tenth of the increase in their herds and flocks. But where there had been heavy losses of such animals because of accidents, he excused the people from paying tribute for three years. If a ship laden with goods had been struck by lightning, he did not collect from it any duties or share of the cargo.

In the city of Canbalu itself the Khan showed great charity toward the poor. If a respectable family had the misfortune to become poor, or because of illness or old age was unable to earn a living, he gave it food and clothing.

This charity was something new. Under the Mongols' original customs, when a poor man applied to them they simply drove him away with abuse. But here Buddhist priests had persuaded the Khan that caring for the poor was a good work. At his court no one who came to ask for food was denied. Not a day passed on which there were not given out great amounts of rice, millet and other goods. Because of this astonishing liberality toward the poor, Marco said, "the people all adored him as a divinity."

The Chinese people themselves impressed Marco very well. He said, "Their conversation is courteous; they salute each other politely, have an air of good breeding, and eat their food with particular cleanliness. To their parents they show the utmost reverence. Should a child happen to act disrespectfully to his parents or neglect to help them in time of need, there is a public court whose special duty it is to punish severely the crime of filial ingratitude.

"The Khan has forbidden all kinds of gambling and other ways of cheating, to which the people of this country are addicted more than any others upon earth. As an argument against the practice, he said to them in an edict, 'I subdued you by the power of my sword, and whatever you possess belongs of right to me: if you gamble, therefore, you are gambling with my property.' He does not, however, take anything arbitrarily in virtue of this right.

"The order observed by all ranks of people, when they come before his majesty, ought not to pass unnoticed. When they approach within half a mile of the place where he happens to be, they show their respect by assuming a humble, placid, and quiet manner. Not the least noise, or the voice of any person calling out, or even speaking aloud, is heard.

"Every man of rank carries with him a small vessel into which he spits, so long as he is in the hall of audience, no one daring to spit on the floor; and when he has spat he replaces the cover and makes a salutation. They take with them handsome boots made of white leather, and when they reach the court, before they enter the hall where they wait a summons from the Khan, they put on these white boots, and give those in which they had walked to the care of the servants. This is so that they will not soil the beautiful carpets, of silk and gold and a variety of colors."

And yet the astrologers had predicted an outbreak of rebellion in Canbalu, and that was why the Khan had built the new capital city across the stream. Most of the Chinese were forced to leave the ancient city and live in the new. But some, whose loyalty he did not suspect, were allowed to remain, because the new city could not hold as many as the old one, which was very much larger.

In spite of this the predicted rebellion broke out while Marco was at the court. It was clear evidence to him that in spite of all the Khan's good works, the Mongol conquerors were hated by the Chinese. He came to understand that since the Khan had become ruler of China not by any legal right, but only by force of arms, he had no confidence in the people. Therefore he put all the provincial governments and magistracies in the hands of Mongols, Arabs, Christians and other foreigners who belonged to his household, and whom he could trust. Because of this his government was universally hated by the people. They found themselves treated as slaves by the Mongols and still worse by the Arabs.

In Canbalu there was a large and handsome palace with many halls. Here sat a high court called Sing, which consisted of twelve noblemen who were responsible only to the Khan himself. This court was in charge of all that had to do with the government of the thirty-four provinces of the empire. It had control of the lands and everything belonging to the state.

Among the members of the court was an Arab named Ahmad, a crafty and bold man, whose influence with the Khan was greater than that of any of the others. "His master," said Marco, "was so infatuated with him that he indulged him in every liberty. It was discovered, indeed, after his death, that he had by means of spells so fascinated his majesty as to oblige him to give ear and credit to whatever he said." So Ahmad was able to act in all matters according to his own will. He gave away all public offices and pronounced judgment upon all offenders. When he wanted to sacrifice any man to whom he bore ill will, he had only to go to the emperor and say to him, "This person has committed an offense against your majesty, and is deserving of death." The emperor would reply, "Do as you judge best," and the man would be immediately executed.

So clear were the proofs of Ahmad's authority and of the Khan's faith in whatever he said, that no one dared to contradict him in anything. Every person, however high in rank or office, stood in awe of him. Even a man accused by Ahmad of murder could not get anyone to defend him because no one dared to oppose the will of Ahmad. Thus many died unjustly. Ahmad had gained great wealth, because everyone who wanted an official job had to make him a large present. He also seized any beautiful young girl to whom he took a fancy and made her one of his many wives.

This had gone on for twenty-two years. At last the Chinese, no longer able to endure the many acts of injustice, held secret meetings to devise ways of putting him to death and raising a rebellion against the government. The leader in this plot was a Chinese officer named Chen-chu, a chief of 6,000 men. He was joined by another Chinese named Van-chu, who was at the head of 10,000 men.

They planned the rebellion for the time when the Khan had gone to his summer palace at Xanadu, and his eldest son Genghis had gone to a summer resort of his own. The Khan had left Ahmad in charge of the city.

The two Chinese revealed their plot to other leaders not only in Canbalu but in other cities. It was decided that on a certain day, when a signal was given by a bonfire, the Chinese would rise up and put to death all who wore beards. Then they would send the signal to other places so that the uprising might spread throughout the country. The reason for killing all who had beards was that the Chinese themselves are naturally beardless, while the Mongols, the Arabs and the Christians wore beards.

First of all, Ahmad must be got rid of. On the chosen night, the two Chinese crossed the stream to Taidu and managed to make their way into the palace, either by bribing the guards or appealing to them as Chinese.

They went to Prince Genghis's rooms and sent a messenger to Ahmad, with the word that the prince had unexpectedly come home and that Ahmad must go to him immediately. Ahmad was much astonished but at once left his house in Canbalu and went to the gate of the new city. There he met a Mongol officer named Kogatai, the commander of the guard of 12,000 men, who asked him where he was going at that late hour. Ahmad replied that he was going to wait upon the prince, of whose arrival he had just heard.

"How is it possible," said the officer, "that he

can have arrived so secretly that I should not have known of his approach in time to order a party of his guards to attend him?" Suspicious, Kogatai followed Ahmad to the door of the prince's room. There Van-chu was sitting on the throne. In the dim light Ahmad supposed Van-chu to be the prince and made his prostrations before him. Chen-chu, who stood there, raised his sword and with a swift stroke cut off the Arab's head. Kogatai cried "Treason!" and raising the bow he carried, let fly an arrow at Van-chu as he sat upon the throne, and killed him instantly. He then called to his men, who seized Chen-chu, and sent an order into the city that every person found out of doors should be put to death.

The Chinese saw that the Mongols had discovered the plot, and one of their leaders being dead and the other a prisoner, they kept within their houses. They were unable to send the signals to the other towns as had been planned.

Kogatai immediately sent messengers to the Khan, with a full story of all that had happened. The Khan sent back an order to investigate the

treason and to punish those concerned. The next day Kogatai examined all the Chinese and put to death all the leaders of the conspiracy.

The Khan returned to Canbalu, anxious to know the causes of what had happened. When he learned how Ahmad and seven of his sons had oppressed the people, he gave orders that the vast fortune which Ahmad had accumulated in his house in the old city was to be seized and put in his own treasury. He also had Ahmad's body taken from the tomb and thrown into the street to be

75

torn to pieces by dogs. The seven sons who had followed the steps of their father in his wickedness he sentenced to be skinned alive.

Because Ahmad and his sons were Arabs, the Khan decided that there must be something wrong with Arab ideas. Marco said that Arabs seemed to think that they had the right to commit crimes or even to murder people who did not agree with them. So the Khan called before him all the Arabs in the capital and ordered them to change their customs. For example, hereafter their marriages must be held under Mongol rules, and in many ways they must live as the Mongols did.

But this was not of much help to the Chinese, who had failed in their rebellion.

10

Hunting

FOUR ELEPHANTS trod northward out of Peking, two abreast. Slung across their broad backs was a pavilion of wood, handsomely carved. It was lined within with cloth of gold, and the outside was covered with the skins of tigers and leopards. In it sat the Khan, on his way to his great spring hunt. He had to ride this way because he had the gout.

In the pavilion also were twelve officers, his favorites, "to keep him company and amuse him," said Marco. He carried with him twelve of his best falcons. Alongside the elephants rode men on horseback, watching the skies for the approach of cranes. When they called out that they spied cranes, the Khan raised the curtains of the pavilion and ordered the falcons let loose. Flying high above the cranes, the falcons swooped down upon them and after a struggle overpowered them.

The Khan took with him on this hunt no less than 10,000 men who acted as falconers, and an uncounted number of falcons and other birds, including vultures, to chase game animals. He also had another 10,000 men to act as watchers. These were sent out in small parties of two or three to posts surrounding a large area. Each of them had a whistle and a hood so that they could call the birds in and secure them. When the command was given for flying the birds, those who let them loose did not have to follow them themselves. It was the watchers' duty to get them wherever they flew. Every bird belonging to the Khan or to any of his nobles, had a small silver label fastened to its leg. On each label were engraved the names of the owner and the keeper.

The Khan's hunting party had a "lost-and-found" system. If the finder of a bird did not know the owner personally, the bird was taken to an officer whose title was "guardian of unclaimed property." If a horse, a sword, or any other article was found, the finder carried it directly to this officer. If a person found any lost article and failed to turn it in, he was regarded as a thief. This lost-and-found officer was always stationed in the highest part of the camp, and flew a special flag, so that

79

he could be found easily. No articles were ever finally lost.

The Khan did not keep his vast body of men together in one place. He divided them into parties of one or two hundred or more. They followed the sport in various directions and brought most of their game to him.

Steadily the hunting party moved toward the ocean shores. Sometimes it came to passes so narrow that only a single elephant could go through. Here the Khan's pavilion must be taken down, and he must ride through on the back of only one elephant.

At night he would make camp under a vast tent, about which were pitched the tents of his sons and the thousands of noblemen, guards and falconers. With the Khan on this hunt were the whole of his family and household, his physicians, his astrologers, and all other officers.

His own tent, in which he gave his audiences, was so long and wide that 10,000 soldiers might be drawn up under it and still leave room for the superior officers and other persons of rank. Its en-

trance faced south. On the eastern side another
tent was connected with it, forming a large room
which the Khan usually occupied, with a few of
his nobility. In the rear of this there was a large
and handsome room where he slept. There were
many other tents for the different branches of the
household, which were not immediately connected
with the great tent. Each of these tents was supported by three pillars of wood, richly carved and
gilt. The tents were covered on the outside with
tiger skins, streaked white, black and red, and so
well joined together that neither wind nor rain
could get in. They were lined with the skins of
ermines and sables, the most costly of all furs.
The tent ropes were of silk. Near the great tent of
the Khan were those of his ladies, also very splendid. The ladies had their own falcons and hawks
with which they joined the pleasures of the hunt.

The people collected in the camp came from
every part of the empire. Their number was so incredible that Marco felt as if he were in the
midst of a great city.

In this hunting region the Khan stayed until

the spring. He often went to the lakes and rivers where he killed or captured storks, swans, herons and other birds. He sent hunters out to many different places, who brought much game back to him. "He enjoyed himself," said Marco, "to a degree that no person who was not an eyewitness could conceive. The excellence of the sport was greater than it is possible to express." Even when it came time for him to return to the capital, he kept up the hunting all the way back.

Every tradesman, workman or farmer throughout his whole dominion was strictly forbidden to keep a vulture, hawk, or any other bird used for the pursuit of game, or any sporting dog. No nobleman could presume to chase a beast or a bird within many miles of where the Khan was, unless his name was on a list kept by the grand falconer. An order prohibited everyone throughout all the countries subject to the Khan, whether prince, nobleman, or peasant, from daring to kill hares, roebucks, fallow deer, stags, or other game animals or any large birds, between the months of March and October. This was so that the game might

increase. Anyone who broke this order was pun-
ished. Therefore game of every kind increased
enormously.

During the months of December, January and
February, when it was too cold to hunt in the
north, the Khan gave orders for hunting parties
to take place in all the country within forty days'
travel from the capital. Governors of districts were
required to send to the court all large game such
as wild boars, stags, fallow deer, roebucks and
bears. All landowners gathered at the places where
these animals were to be found, and surrounded
them. Then the animals were killed, some by
dogs, but chiefly by shooting them with arrows.
Animals for the Khan's use were gutted and sent
on carts, in large quantities, by those who were
within thirty days' journey of the capital. Those
who were farther away did not send the carcasses,
but only the skins, some dressed and others raw,
for the use of the army.

The Khan kept many leopards and lynxes and
tigers for the purpose of chasing deer, boars, wild
oxen and asses, bears, stags, roebucks, and other

beasts. When a tiger was let loose, Marco was thrilled to see the savage eagerness and speed with which it overtook its prey. The Khan had his tigers kept in cages placed upon carts. With each was confined a little dog, with which it became familiar. Marco noticed that the tigers were released from a direction opposite to the wind, so that the game would not scent them. The Khan also had eagles trained to swoop at wolves. These were so large and strong that no wolf, however large, could escape their talons.

The Khan had in his service two brothers named Bayan and Mingan, who were "masters of the chase," in charge of the hounds. Each of them had under his orders a body of 10,000 huntsmen. Those under one brother wore red uniforms, and those under the other sky-blue. The dogs which they took to the field numbered 5,000. One brother, with his dogs, took the ground on the right of the emperor, and the other took the left. Each advanced in regular order until they surrounded a tract of country as wide as would be covered in a day's march. By this means no beast could escape them.

"It was a beautiful and an exhilarating sight," said Marco, "to watch the exertions of the huntsmen and the skill of the dogs, when the emperor was within the circle, engaged in the sport, and they were seen chasing the stags, bears, and other animals in every direction." The two brothers were required to supply the court daily, from the first of October to the end of March, with a thousand pieces of game. They also had to supply fish in as large a quantity as possible.

Marco took great pleasure in recording these many details of the hunting parties of the Khan and his officers.

But there was more serious and more violent business ahead.

11

The Battle

KUBLAI, the sixth in the line of the Khans which had begun with Genghis, had become the greatest of them. He held power over more lands, more people and more treasure—"surpassing," Marco said, "every ruler there ever has been or now is in the world." It was natural that he had jealous rivals.

Before Kublai had come to the throne, he had served in the Mongol army. He had shown himself brave and bold in battle and in military skill.

He was called the most able and successful commander who ever led the Mongols.

For many years now he had not taken the field in person. Expeditions were left to his sons and other generals.

But during Marco's stay there was such a serious outbreak that the Khan put himself at the head of his armies and went out to fight a great battle.

His armies were mighty. In every region there were leaders who were not loyal to the Khan, and there was always danger that the conquered

87

Chinese might rise up in rebellion against their Mongol emperor. Therefore the Khan kept up armies far and wide. They were in constant readiness in camps a few miles from every large city. These armies and their commanders were changed about every two years. "If even half of these armies were to gather in one place," Marco said, "their numbers would be almost incredible."

Now the Khan had need of a large part of his forces.

He had placed a kinsman of his, whose name was Nayan, in command of the armies in the north, in Korea, Manchuria and Mongolia. These added up to 400,000 horsemen. Nayan was only thirty years old. "Upon finding himself at the head of so great a force, he was affected by youthful vanity," sternly said Marco, who was himself so much younger. Nayan laid a plot to seize the throne for himself.

In the far west, in Turkestan, there was that other powerful relative of the Khan named Kaidu. Marco had heard about him when he first entered western China on his journey some years before.

The Khan had beaten Kaidu but had still left him in command of his 100,000 horsemen. Nayan, knowing that Kaidu was angry, now secretly sent messengers to him, proposing that he join the uprising. Kaidu agreed. Both chieftains began to gather their forces.

Such a vast mobilization could not go on without the news of it coming to the ear of the Khan. He immediately sent out troops to occupy the mountain passes leading to the north and west. Then he gave orders that all of his armies within ten days' march of the capital should be quickly assembled. These amounted to 360,000 horsemen and 100,000 foot soldiers. Among them were the Khan's personal bodyguard of 12,000 horsemen, who usually did duty at the palace, and also his 10,000 falconers. Within twenty days all were ready.

The Khan's plan was to strike at Nayan before Kaidu could join him. By forced marches, day and night, he reached Nayan's region in twenty-five days.

Marco rode with the troops. They came at last

to a range of hills, beyond which stretched the plain where Nayan's army lay encamped. The Mongols always chose to fight in open, level country, where their swift horsemen could gallop to the attack. Behind the hills Kublai halted his troops and allowed them two days of rest.

No word of his approach reached Nayan. All passes and roads had been kept so tightly closed that no courier or spy could get through.

While his men were resting, the Khan called upon his astrologers to prophesy which side would win. Of course the astrologers said that the Khan would be the victor. This cheerful news was proclaimed to the whole army. The troops were confident of victory. Early in the morning, they swept over the last hill and down into the plain.

The attack was a complete surprise. Nayan was asleep in his tent, and his army was carelessly posted, without any scouts or advance parties on the watch.

The Khan rode to battle in a large wooden castle, borne on the backs of four elephants. The bodies of the elephants were protected by coverings of thick leather hardened by fire. Over the leather were housings of cloth of gold. Surrounding the Khan as he sat in the castle were many cross-bowmen and archers. Above them flew the imperial flag, on which were designs showing the sun and moon.

In the Khan's front line were thirty battalions of horsemen. Each battalion contained 10,000 men armed with bows and arrows. In front of each battalion of horsemen were placed 500 foot soldiers armed with short lances and swords. These men were trained to leap up behind the riders when they charged, and when they reached the enemy, they would jump off and kill with their lances the enemy's horses.

The Khan spread his left and right wings so far as to outflank his enemy. Nayan, wakened, hastily formed his troops as best he could.

It was the Mongol custom in warfare, first, to form the line of battle, second, to sound many horns of various kinds, third, to break into song, and finally, to start a beating of cymbals and great kettle-drums. "It was wonderful to hear," said Marco.

The beating of the drums and cymbals was the

signal to start fighting. A fierce and bloody conflict began. Marco's eyewitness account was vivid. "The air was instantly filled with a cloud of arrows that poured down on every side. Vast numbers of men and horses fell to the ground. When their arrows were gone, the hostile sides engaged in close combat with their lances, swords and maces shod with iron. Such was the slaughter, and so large were the heaps of the bodies of men and horses, that it became impossible for either side to advance upon the other. Thus the fortune of the day remained for a long time undecided. Victory wavered between the two armies from morning until noon. Nayan had been most liberal and indulgent toward his people. As a result they were so devoted to him that they were all ready to meet death rather than turn their backs to the enemy. At last, however, Nayan, seeing that he was nearly surrounded, tried to save himself by flight. But he was soon made a prisoner and taken to the presence of Kublai, who gave orders that he be put to death."

The execution was a strange one. Nayan was laid upon a carpet, and another carpet was thrown over him. Then both carpets were picked up by a number of strong men and violently shaken until Nayan was literally shaken to death. This, Marco learned, was so that the sun and the air should not witness the shedding of the blood of one who belonged to the imperial family.

Those of Nayan's troops who survived were made to swear allegiance to the Khan.

Each of the Khan's generals who had commanded 100,000 men was rewarded with a large golden tablet bearing this inscription: "By the power and might of the great God, and through the grace which he vouchsafes to our empire, be the name of the Khan blessed; and let all such as disobey what is herein directed suffer death and be utterly destroyed." Beneath this were inscribed the duties and powers of the commander and his privileges. Among the privileges were these: Whenever he rode in public, an umbrella would be carried over his head to denote his rank and authority. When he was seated, it would always be upon a silver chair. He could also make use of the horses of the imperial stud whenever he wished.

12

The Conquest of Burma

THE USE of elephants had been learned by the Khan some time after Marco's arrival at the court. "A memorable battle," as he called it, had been fought in the far southwest. Marco had been still too young to take part in that expedition, but he heard of it and later put it into his book.

Fearing an attack from the king of Burma, which lay to the south of his dominions, the Khan had sent an army to protect the border. The southern king learned of this and determined to make his attack as soon as possible. He collected a large army and marched north to the place now known in China as Paoshan. Besides 60,000 cavalry and foot soldiers he had many elephants. Upon the back of each elephant was a wooden castle, large enough to hold twelve or sixteen men.

The Khan's general, Nasruddin, was a brave and able officer. But he felt worried because he had only 12,000 men, though they were all veteran soldiers.

He did not give any signs of fear as he led them down into the plain. He took a position near a thick wood of large trees. In case of a furious

charge by the elephants, his troops could retire into the woods and from there shoot their arrows.

When the King of Burma heard that the Mongols had reached the plain, he ordered his army to move toward them. He took up his position about a mile away and placed the elephants in the front line. Behind them were the cavalry and the infantry, in two wide wings. He was very confident. He shouted out to his men that the Mongols were outnumbered five to one. Besides that, they had never been attacked by armed elephants. Then he gave orders for the vast number of horns to be sounded and advanced boldly.

Meanwhile the Khan's men had dug themselves in, in trenches. They waited until the attackers were close, and then rushed out with great spirit for the fight. But the Mongol horses, which had never seen such huge animals, with the castles on their backs, were terrified. They wheeled about and began to run. As soon as the Mongol commander saw this disorder, he ordered his men to dismount and lead their horses into the woods and tie them to the trees. Then the dismounted men immediately started on foot toward the line of elephants, and began a brisk fire of arrows.

The soldiers who were high up in the castles on the elephants' backs, and the rest of the king's army, shot volleys of arrows in return. But their arrows were not as deadly as those of the Mongols, whose bows were drawn with stronger arms. The commander ordered that all the arrows be aimed at the elephants. These were soon covered with arrows. Suddenly they gave way and fell back upon the soldiers behind them, who were thrown into confusion. It was impossible for their drivers to manage them. Smarting under the pain of their wounds, and terrified by the shouting of the Mongols, the elephants went out of control and ran about in all directions. At last, filled with rage and fear, they rushed into a part of the wood not occupied by the Mongols. The trees were large and the branches close together. The castles on the elephants' backs broke, with loud crashes. All the men who sat on them were killed or injured.

When they saw the rout of the elephants, the Mongols took fresh courage. Marching off in perfect order, one detachment after another, they untied and remounted their horses and joined their divisions. Then came bloody and dreadful combat. The troops of Burma were brave enough, and their king went among the ranks urging them to stand firm, and not be alarmed by what had happened to the elephants. But the Mongols, by their great skill in archery, were too powerful for them. The Burmese did not have heavy armor such as the Mongols wore.

Soon both sides had shot all their arrows. Then they grasped their swords and iron maces, and there was violent hand-to-hand fighting. The King of Burma, a valiant chief, rushed to the place of greatest danger, encouraging his soldiers and begging them to stand their ground. At last he saw that it was impossible any longer to keep up the conflict or to stand against the furious Mongols. Most of his troops were either killed or wounded. The field was covered with the bodies of men and horses. Those who were still on their feet were beginning to retreat. The king at last saw that he must take flight with the wreck of his army. Many more were slain afterward by the pursuing Mongols.

This battle had lasted from morning till noon. The Mongol victory, as Marco studied it, was due to several factors. First, the troops of the King of Burma did not wear armor as the Mongols did. Second, their elephants, also without armor, had no defense against the Mongol arrows. Otherwise they would have broken into the Mongol ranks and thrown them into disorder.

A third point, perhaps of still greater importance as Marco saw it, was that the king ought not to have made his attack in a position where the Mongol flank was supported by the woods. He should have tried to draw them into the open country, where they could not have resisted the first onset of the armed elephants and where he might have surrounded them by his two wings of cavalry.

After the slaughter of the enemy, the Mongols returned to the woods into which the elephants had fled and took possession of them. With the help of survivors who knew how to manage the elephants, they captured about two hundred. "Ever since this battle," said Marco, "the Khan has chosen to use elephants in his armies."

What was more important to Marco personally, was that as a result of the victory the Khan took possession of the entire territory held by the King of Burma, and annexed it to his dominions. For now, some years later, Marco was sent as the Khan's ambassador to Burma and other regions in the southwest.

The Khan knew that many of his own people, and the Chinese whom he had conquered, were not always to be trusted. Therefore, he often chose for important tasks persons of foreign lands. One of these had been the wicked Ahmad, who had been assassinated in the palace. Others were Jews and Christians.

Now Marco, the young Christian from Venice, had grown to maturity. He had won the confidence of the Khan. And so he was chosen for this responsible mission to the southwest, on which he was to be gone for many months.

13

The Burma Road

MARCO RODE westward out of Peking. At the end
of ten miles he came to a river, spanned by a handsome stone bridge. Here, many years before, a
mutiny of Chinese soldiers had opened the way
for Genghis Khan to capture Peking. And to us of
modern times Marco's crossing of this bridge was
a memorable beginning of his journey. For it was
there, too, that the last war between China and
Japan began on July 7, 1937. It is called the
"Marco Polo" bridge because he described it,

more than six hundred years ago, very much as we see it today, although twice it has had to be restored.

Turning toward the south Marco rode on, day after day. He stopped by night at inns. Everywhere he made notes of the habits of the people and the things they produced. Gold tissues and the finest gauze. Vineyards and wine. Silk spun by worms that fed on the leaves of mulberry trees. Bamboo, which he found was used for various purposes. Ginger, spikenard and many useful drugs.

He was pleased by the high civilization of the Chinese. He liked the way the country people kept in touch with the towns, and the towns, being close together, kept in touch with one another. They held many fairs for mutual trade. All this was quite different from what he had seen in his travels across the mountains and deserts. But even here, in the hills beyond the towns, there were wild animals—tigers, bears, lynxes, fallow deer, antelopes, stags.

After many pleasant days Marco came to the "large and noble" city of Chengtu, "formerly the seat of many rich and powerful kings." The outer walls of the city were twenty miles around, but it was walled off into three sections. The former king had had three sons. He wanted each of them to reign after his death, and so he divided the city among them. When the three brothers became kings, each had also for his portion a large tract of country outside the walls. But the Mongol invaders had come and captured the region. They put the three kings to death, and the Khan had taken all their riches for himself.

Many streams flowing down from the mountains passed through the city in several directions. Some of these rivers were half a mile wide, others narrow and very deep. Marco was struck by the covered bridges which crossed some of the streams. Built of stone, each bridge had from one end to the other a row of marble pillars on each side. These supported the handsome roofs, made of wood, ornamented with red paint and covered with tiles. The bridges were filled for their whole length with little buildings and shops, where all sorts of trades were carried on. In one of the buildings were officers who collected the customs duties on food and goods, and a toll from everyone who crossed the bridge. In this way the Khan took a large daily income from the people.

After leaving Chengtu, Marco traveled along close to the border of that fabulous country, Tibet. Wild beasts, especially tigers, made travel dangerous along this border. He was taught how to protect his horses against attack while he camped at night. In this region, and particularly along rivers, grew large bamboo trees. Marco learned to cut these, while still green, tie several together, put them at some distance from his tents and build a fire under them. When darkness came on, he lighted the fire. When it became hot, the bamboos would burst with tremendous explosions. The noise was so loud that it could be heard for two miles and would terrify the wild beasts and make them fly from the neighborhood. He learned also that his horses must be fastened with heavy iron shackles, so that when they too were frightened by the noise, they could not break their halters and run away. Many travelers who neglected to do this lost their horses.

For twenty days Marco pressed on through desolate country, where there were no inns. Once in three or four days he would reach a market where he could buy a stock of food and supplies. At the end of the third week he began to see a few castles and strong towns, built on rocky heights, or even on the summits of mountains. Then gradually he came to peaceful villages and farms and was no longer in any danger from beasts of prey.

Back again in more civilized country, he began to make notes on a subject which always interested him as the son of a Venetian merchant—the various things used for money. Here he was outside of the region where the Khan's clever use of paper money was known. In Tibet, he heard, the money was red coral, brought perhaps from the shores of India. The women wore necklaces of coral and used it to ornament their idols.

Further on he came to a place where salt was

money. Here there was a large lake of salt water, and many salt springs. The water was boiled in small pans for an hour. Then it became a kind of paste which was molded into small cakes, flat on the bottom and rounded on the top. These were placed on hot tiles near a fire to dry and harden. No one was allowed to make these cakes except officers appointed by the Khan. They pressed upon them the stamp of the grand Khan.

Finally, after crossing a great river, Marco found a place where the money was white porcelain shells brought up river from the sea. As with the coral, these valuable sea shells were also worn as necklaces.

The river was the mighty Yangtze, "the river of the golden sands."

Marco soon noticed a sharp difference between the peoples of northern and of southern China, a difference which is still seen today, 600 years later. He said, "The land is fertile in rice and wheat. The people, however, do not eat wheaten bread, which they think is unwholesome. *They eat rice,* and of the other grain, with the addition of spices, they make wine."

Traveling still southwestward he came to the great lake of Tali. Here he was amazed by his discovery of crocodiles. It has to be admitted that he did not describe them very accurately. Here is what he said: "At the fore-part, near the head, they have two short legs, having three claws like those of a tiger, with eyes larger than a fourpenny loaf and very glaring. The jaws are wide enough to swallow a man, the teeth are large and sharp, and their whole appearance is so terrible that neither man, nor any kind of animal, can approach them without fear. Some are smaller and the following method is used for capturing them. In the daytime, because of the great heat, they lurk in caverns. At night, they go out to seek their food. Whatever beast they meet and can lay hold of, whether tiger, wolf, or any other, they devour. Then they drag themselves toward some lake, spring, or river in order to drink. By their motion in this way along the shore, and their vast weight, they make a deep impression, as if a heavy beam had been drawn along the sands. Those whose work it is to hunt them observe the track by which they usually go, and fix into the ground several pieces of wood, armed with sharp iron spikes, which they cover with the sand so that it cannot be seen. When the animals make their way toward the places they haunt, they are wounded by these instruments, and speedily killed. The crows, as soon as they see them to be dead, set up their scream. This serves as a signal to the hunters, who go to the spot, and proceed to separate the skin from the flesh. They take care immediately to secure the gall, which is most highly valued in medicine. The flesh of the animal is sold at a high price, for it is thought to have a greater flavor than other kinds of meat, and everyone considers it a delicacy."

Marco was also interested in the horses here. They were large and were sent all the way to India for sale. One joint of the tail was removed to keep the horse from lashing it from side to side, and to make it hang straight down. "Whisking it about, in riding, appears to these people a vile habit," said Marco.

His sharp eye noticed that the people rode with long stirrups, "as the French do in our part of the world." The Mongols wore their stirrups short, so that they could rise high above their saddles when they shot their arrows.

He was now drawing near to the border where the great battle had been fought, and he was traveling the route which was to become famous in World War II as the "Burma Road."

More and more of what he saw seemed so strange to him that he recorded it quite fully. Thus we can recognize customs which still exist 600 years later. For example, he wrote: "Both the men and the women of this province have the custom of covering their teeth with thin plates of gold, which are fitted with great exactness to the shape of their teeth, and always stay on them. The men form dark stripes or bands around their arms and legs, by puncturing them in the following manner. They have five needles joined together, which they press into the flesh until blood is drawn. They then rub the punctures with a black coloring matter, which leaves an indelible mark. To bear these dark stripes is considered as an ornamental and honorable distinction." Such tattooing is known even today among the tribes in that region.

He discovered an extreme form of ancestor worship. "In this district," he reported, "they have neither temples nor idols, but pay their worship to the elder or ancestor of the family. From him they say they derive their existence, so they are indebted to him for all that they possess."

In a rough mountain area, covered with thick forests, he found the deadly malaria which even during World War II killed so many workers on the Burma Road. "During the summer," he wrote, "the atmosphere is so gloomy and unwholesome that traders and other strangers have to leave the district in order to escape death."

His description of the Burma Road is unmistakable. "You enter upon a vast descent, which you travel for two days and a half, in the course of which no habitations are found. Beyond this, in a southerly direction, toward the borders of India, lies the city of Mien. The journey takes fifteen days, through a country much depopulated, and forests filled with elephants, rhinoceroses, and other wild beasts."

Passing among people who had no doctors, he was shocked by the way they were cheated by sorcerers. When a person of wealth was taken ill, his family sent for the sorcerers. They called out people with drums and horns to play and dance and sing in praise of their idols. They kept this up loudly until, as the sorcerers said, the "evil spirit" entered into one of them. Then the music stopped, and the sorcerers asked the person with the evil spirit what was the cause of the man's illness and how to cure him. The evil spirit answered through the mouth of the man whose body he had entered that the cause of the sickness was an offense given to a certain god. The sorcerers then prayed to that god, begging him to forgive the sinner on the condition that when he was cured he would offer a sacrifice. If the evil spirit believed that there was no hope of the man's recovery, he said the god was

so very much offended that no sacrifice could sat-
isfy him. But if he thought that a cure was likely
anyway, he demanded an offering of a number of
sheep, and that a certain number of sorcerers be
assembled to perform the sacrifice. The relations
immediately did all that was demanded. The
sheep were slain, and their blood was sprinkled
toward the heavens. The sorcerers lighted up
and perfumed with incense the house of the sick
person, making a smoke with wood of aloes.
They laughed, sang and danced about, doing
honor to their god. Then they asked the evil
spirit whether the sacrifice satisfied the god or if
he commanded another. When the answer was
that he was satisfied, the sorcerers sat down at the
table and proceeded to feast on the meat that had
been offered in sacrifice and to drink the spiced
liquor. Having finished their meal and received
their fees, they returned to their homes.

If the patient recovered, they would give credit
for his cure to the god for whom they had per-
formed. If the patient happened to die, they would
then declare that the rites had been spoiled be-

cause someone who had dressed the meat had dared to taste it before the god's portion had been presented to him. "And thus," said the pious Marco, "do the demons sport with the blindness of the deluded and the wretched."

Finally Marco came to the end of his extraordinary expedition at the great and magnificent city called Mien. There he saw a memorial erected in honor of a former king. When he knew his death was drawing near, that rich and powerful monarch gave orders for erecting at the head and foot of his tomb two great towers of marble, each with a ball on top. One of these pyramids was entirely covered with a plating of gold an inch thick and the other with silver of the same thickness. Around the two balls were hung small gold and silver bells, which sounded when shaken by the wind. The tomb also was covered with gold and silver.

When Kublai Khan's army had come to take possession of the city and had seen the two pyramids so richly ornamented, the commander dared not meddle with them until his emperor's wishes were known. When the Khan heard that they had been put up in memory of a former king, he ordered that they should not be damaged in any way. For the Mongols thought it a serious sin to remove anything that belonged to the dead.

His mission in Mien ended, Marco turned northward to return to the capital. Varying his route, he veered eastward through Indo-China. There the people spoke a different language, but they sent an annual tribute to the Khan. There, too, both men and women had their bodies tattooed all over with figures of beasts and birds. The man or woman who had the most figures was thought the most handsome.

At Ami Marco recorded that "both men and women wear rings of gold and silver on their wrists, arms and legs; but those of the females are the more costly."

Before he got back to the road by which he had come, he had a final exciting discovery—tiger hunting. He came to a place where there were so many tigers that the people never dared to sleep at night outside of the towns. Boatmen on the river did not dare to go to rest with their boats moored near the banks. Tigers had been known to plunge into the water, swim to the vessel and drag men off. So the vessels were anchored in the middle of the stream, too far out for the tigers to reach them.

The hunters had the largest and fiercest dogs that Marco had ever seen. A man with two of these dogs and armed with a bow and arrows, was a match for a tiger. When he met a tiger, he set on his courageous dogs. The tiger instinctively sought a tree against which to place himself so that the dogs could not get behind him, and he

would have his foe in front. As soon as he saw the dogs, he moved toward the tree at a slow pace. A tiger's pride would not allow him to show any sign of fear. Before he could reach the tree, the dogs were upon him. He turned and tried to claw the dogs, but they were too quick for him and drew back. He took up his slow march again. Meanwhile the hunter was shooting arrow after arrow into the tiger. Wounded by so many arrows, and so often bitten by the dogs, he fell at last through weakness and loss of blood. The hunters carried his body home in triumph.

14

Down the Grand Canal

WHEN MARCO had first arrived at the court, Kublai Khan had not yet finished his conquest of all China. To the south of the wide Yellow River and stretching from the mountains to the sea, lay a vast, rich country. It was still ruled by a Chinese emperor, "the Son of Heaven." His ancestors had governed most of China for more than six hundred years. These are known in history as the Sung dynasty. A century and a half before, after much bitter warfare in the north, one of the royal princes had fled to the south and built a new capital at Hangchow. It was this capital that the Mongols now set out to capture.

The Sung emperor was a peaceful man. "He had never seen a battle," said Marco. "He was a friend to peace and justice." Travelers of all sorts could pass through every part of his kingdom, by night as well as by day, freely and without any danger. He was religious and charitable to the poor, and he was beloved by all his people Everybody thought that his kingdom was safe, because it was sheltered by great rivers and broken up by much water. It was not like the open plains of the north, where the fleet horses of the hard-riding Mongols could lead the attack. The Chinese emperor did not keep up any cavalry at all. He simply surrounded his cities with deep ditches the width of a bow-shot, so that his archers could defend them.

"Very different from the temper and habits of the Son of Heaven," said Marco, "were those of Kublai Khan, emperor of the Mongols, whose whole delight consisted in thoughts of a warlike nature, of the conquest of countries, and of increasing his fame."

The Khan collected a large army and put it under the command of a general named Chin-san Bayan. This name meant "Hundred-Eyes." A great fleet of ships carried the army across the wide Yellow River and landed on the southern shores. At the first walled city he came to, "Hundred-Eyes" called for surrender, but was defied. Not pausing to attack he went on past three other cities which also refused to yield. He then decided that it was not wise to leave so many cities in his rear. He attacked the next one, and when his forces broke into it they killed every man, woman and child. The news of this Mongol terror ran ahead of him and all the other cities in the path gave up without resistance. But the great capital at Hangchow still lay ahead.

Hangchow is near the sea, and the Chinese emperor had a fleet of ships ready. He loaded them with all his personal treasure and went aboard and sailed to a distant island which was strongly fortified. There he lived for the rest of his life.

He had given orders that the city should be defended and left his empress in command. He thought that being a woman she would be safe even if she fell into the hands of the enemy. After he was at sea, the empress learned of the astrologers' prediction. They said the emperor could never be overthrown except by a chief with a hundred eyes. This gave her confidence. But next she was told that the general who was besieging the city was Chin-san Bayan, or "Hundred-Eyes." Terrified by this, she immediately surrendered. Marco saw with satisfaction that she was sent to Kublai Khan, who ordered an allowance paid to her, "enough to support the splendid dignity of her rank."

After the capture of Hangchow the Mongols had no trouble in taking control of the rest of the kingdom. And now Kublai Khan reigned over the greatest empire that the world has ever known.

Yet he was not satisfied. Eastward of his dominions lay a part of the ocean which was called the Sea of Chin. In writing down this word Marco came as near as he ever did to the modern name of China. He called the northern regions which he had first seen "Cathay" and the newly conquered south "Manji."

Sailors and traders who crossed the Sea of Chin brought back tales of a great island called Zipangu. This, of course, was Japan. They said that it was very rich in gold and precious stones and pearls. The king's palace had a roof of pure gold. Excited by these stories, the Khan decided that he must add Japan to his possessions. Now that the war for the south was won, he fitted out a large fleet of ships, filled it with troops and sent it across the sea. The expedition reached Japan safely and landed soldiers who captured one city, where as was their custom, they put everyone to death.

Soon afterward a north wind began to blow with great force. Meeting in council, the officers decided that they ought to get the ships away from the shore. They took the troops on board and headed out to sea. But the gale grew still more violent and a number of the vessels were wrecked. Thirty thousand men, floating on pieces of wreckage, reached a barren island about four miles from the main coast of Japan. The ships which escaped the storm, and on which all the principal officers were, returned home.

The shipwrecked Mongols on the island found themselves left without ships, abandoned by their leaders, and with no arms or provisions. The island did not even offer any shelter. As soon as the gale ceased and the sea became smooth and calm, a large force of Japanese in many boats sailed over from the main island to take the Mongols prisoners. They landed and started in search of them. The Mongols had concealed themselves behind some high land in the center of the island. While the enemy were hurrying in pursuit of them by one road, they made their way down along the coast by another. This brought them to the place where a fleet of boats lay at anchor. The boats were all unarmed, but Japanese flags were still flying. The Mongols instantly boarded them, and pushing off from the island, sailed straight for the principal harbor of Japan. Not suspected because of the flags, they were allowed to sail in unopposed. Ashore, they drove out the people of the

city. The Japanese ruler immediately ordered a blockade which was so strict that no one was allowed to enter or leave the city. For six months the siege continued. At the end of that time, the Mongols gave up hope of rescue and surrendered on the condition that their lives be spared.

It was several years before the Khan learned all that had happened to his lost expedition. And it must have been a great disappointment to Marco that he was never able to get to Japan.

Marco also learned from sailors—"to whom the truth must be known," he said—that beyond the Sea of Chin there were more than seven thousand islands, mostly inhabited. It was said of the trees which grew on them that every one yielded a fragrant smell. They came to be called "The Spice Islands." Marco said wistfully that he could not tell about the islands. They were so far away that he could not visit them personally, and they were not under the rule of the Khan.

But Marco could visit the conquered lands of Manji on the mainland. When he did so, he was astonished by their magnificence and wealth, which were far greater than he had seen before. He admired even more the gentle, civilized ways of these people who had lived for so many generations under peaceful rulers before the Mongols came. Theirs was a civilization finer than any he had ever known. He made his notes about it with loving care.

Marco crossed into Manji over a handsome stone causeway, the only road into that southern region. On both sides of the causeway there were large lakes, deep enough to be navigated. Now he saw how the Khan's forces under "Hundred-Eyes" had made their invasion; this was how they were able to land so large an army. He saw, too, great numbers of ships passing up and down the river. There was much trade in silk and gold tissues, and there were great saltworks, which paid large taxes to the Khan.

Now Marco was traveling along the Grand Canal. This was a deep inland waterway dug by the Khan's orders. It linked his capital in the north with the cities of the south. Lakes and rivers were connected by the canal so that large vessels could go all the way without once having to put to sea. Thus the rich tribute which the Khan forced the south to pay, in taxes and all kinds of goods, could be brought to him safely. And the people could also trade among themselves more freely than before.

Both banks of the canal were wide roads, made of the earth thrown up when the canal was dug, so these could be traveled easily on foot or horseback or with carts filled with goods for sale.

The Grand Canal led to the Yangtze River. This seemed to Marco "the largest river in the world." At some places, he heard, it was ten miles wide. Its length was more than 3,000 miles. Marco said that at one town he saw as many as 15,000 vessels. He noticed that each of these had a deck and a mast with one sail. Many of them were towed along the banks by horses, ten or twelve for each boat. The ropes by which they were towed were made of split bamboo, twisted.

He saw standing up from the river a tall, steep island, or rock. On this was a great temple and monastery, where 200 monks lived. If you go up the Yangtze River today, you can still see that rocky island at the place where it meets the Grand Canal. It is called Golden Island, and on it are many old temples and above all, a handsome pagoda.

Behind Marco, as he stood on the northern shore of the Yangtze River, lay the city of Yangchow through which he had just passed. This was an important city. Arms and all sorts of equipment for war were manufactured there, and many soldiers were stationed in and about it.

At the capital Marco had learned of the court of twelve noblemen appointed by the Khan to govern the various parts of his empire. One of these noblemen was stationed at Yangchow. He was in charge of a large region which included twenty-four towns. And the time was to come when Marco himself, "by special order of the Khan," was to take the place of this governor. For three years the young man from Venice was governor of this key district of Yangchow.

15

The City of Heaven

MARCO WAS ferried across the broad river to Chinkiang. The Grand Canal began again on the other side. Following it he rode on southward, seeing more and more signs of the wealth of this peaceful land. By the time he came to the lovely city of Soochow he had made up his mind about something.

He had been torn between two feelings. He admired the powerful Khan who was now his master. But he also admired the old civilization of the Chinese people. He had seen their ability in making and selling all sorts of things. "There are some very rich merchants among them," he remarked. But he could not help thinking that if they had been as manly and warlike as they were clever, they would never have been conquered.

There were so many of them! After his travels through lands where people were few and far between, he was astonished by the numbers of the Chinese, and by their varied skills. In Soochow he saw that they had a great many doctors who knew much about diseases and drugs. They had many philosophers, followers of the sage Confucius, who had given his teachings five hundred years before Christ.

Soochow was the center of sixteen rich cities and towns, where trade and arts flourished. He was told that it was called "the city of the earth," while the next large city, Hangchow, was "the city of heaven."

For four days Marco passed through pleasant towns and villages. Everywhere the people were well fed and busy at their work. He saw many weaving silk of the finest quality.

Then he came to Hangchow. This city was only one week's journey from Yangchow, where later he was to stay for three years as governor. Therefore he often visited it. He became convinced that it was the best city in the world, in wealth and beauty. "Its abundant delights," he said, "might lead one who lived there to imagine himself in paradise." He made more notes in Hangchow than in any other place he ever visited. What he told about it after he went back to Venice was as tempting to Europeans as what he told of Kublai Khan's courts. When Christopher Columbus read Marco's book he began to dream not only of the grandeur of northern Cathay, and of the fragrant "Spice Islands," but also of the riches of Hangchow.

Hangchow, the "City of Heaven," lay between a beautiful lake and a large river. The river flowed down to the fine seaport of Ningpo, to which seagoing ships brought cargoes from India. The lake was three or four miles wide. Behind it, on three sides, mountains loomed. Along the shore between

Hangchow was called the City of Heaven.

lake and mountains were many great houses and gardens belonging to families of wealth and high rank. Scattered among these were temples filled with monks. On the hills behind stood tall pagodas.

Near the center of the lake were two islands, on each of which was a superb building put up by the people of the city. These buildings had many pavilions, each fitted out with everything needed for great entertainments such as the celebration of a wedding. Sometimes as many as a hundred feasts would be going on at the same time, in separate pavilions, without any one of them interfering with the others.

Floating on the lake were many barges which were also used for parties. Each barge would hold from ten to twenty persons. They were broad and flat-bottomed so that they would not tip as they moved through the water. On a flat upper deck, boatmen walked steadily from bow to stern and back again with long poles which they thrust into the bottom of the shallow lake to propel the boat. Beneath were gaily decorated cabins, set with tables and chairs for feasting. As the boat glided along, the guests could watch on one side the changing beauties of mountains, lake and shoreline. On the other side they could see the whole length of the city in all the beauty of its palaces and gardens, with great trees growing down to the water's edge.

The city itself was large and crowded. Canals connected with the river ran through every part of it as in Venice. The canals were crossed by thousands of bridges. The bridges over the main canals had arches so high that vessels with masts could sail under them, while carts and horses were passing overhead, up and down gentle slopes from the street.

The streets were all paved with stones and bricks, and so were the principal roads leading out from the city. Marco remarked, "Passengers can travel to every part of the province without soiling their feet." For the use of the Khan's couriers, who went on horseback at great speed, a part of the road, on one side, was left unpaved.

The long main street which ran straight from

one end of the city to the other, was paved on each side, but the middle was covered with small gravel, and had drains to carry rain water off into the canals, so that it was always dry. On this gravel road long covered carriages were continually passing. They had silken curtains and cushions, and each had room for six persons. Many people, both men and women, hired carriages for a pleasure drive every day. At every hour there were many of them rolling along the middle of the street, past the many fine houses and gardens, past the thousands of shops, past the great market places.

There were ten market places, large squares facing on the main street. Parallel to the street, opposite the squares, ran a very large canal. On the nearer bank were big stone warehouses for the goods which were brought for sale from as far away as India. In each market place, three days a week, there would gather forty or fifty thousand people. They came with their carts or in their boats to buy and sell food. There was much game —roebucks, stags, fallow deer, rabbits, partridges,

pheasants, quails, common fowls, ducks and geese
that were reared on the lake. There were cuts of
beef and lamb for the tables of the rich. At all
seasons the markets had a great variety of herbs
and fruits, and especially very large fragrant and
delicious peaches, both yellow and white. From the
lake and up the river from the sea came daily a
vast amount of fish. Each of the ten market squares
was bordered with shops, where many kinds of
goods were made and sold.

Among the hand crafts in the city, there were
twelve considered the most useful, and for each of
these there were a thousand workshops. Each shop
employed from ten to forty workmen. The owners
were rich men who did not work with their own
hands. Under ancient laws made by the emperors
each man had to follow the trade of his father. But
when they became rich they could give up manual
labor, as long as they kept the business and hired
others to work at it. They became gentlemen, and
their wives, who did no work either, became ladies
The women were very beautiful. They were
brought up, as Marco put it, with "delicate and

languid habits." They wore costly clothes of silk, and much jewelry. These families built fine houses, and spent a great deal of money on carved ornaments and paintings.

Marco had high praise for the people of Hangchow. They were cordial to strangers who came to do business, inviting them into their homes and giving them their best help and advice. They were naturally peaceable, calm and quiet. In this they followed the example of their former emperors. They knew nothing about the use of weapons and never kept any in their houses. Loud quarreling was never heard among them. They were completely honest and frank in business. They were friendly toward each other, and neighbors living in the same street, both men and women, seemed to be like one family. In their homes the men showed great respect for their wives—never jealousy or suspicion. They seemed to like everybody except soldiers. Especially they disliked the sight of the Khan's guards because they never forgot that it was the Mongols who had overthrown their own rulers.

One of the Khan's nine viceroys lived and held his court in Hangchow. He had authority over more than a hundred and forty cities and towns, all large and rich. In each of these was a garrison of a thousand, or ten, or twenty thousand men. Not many of these troops were Mongols. The Mongols were horsemen, and cavalry could be stationed only on firm, dry ground, where the horses could be used and exercised. To cities in low, marshy places the Khan sent Chinese soldiers chosen for their fighting ability. But he never placed them near their homes. He marched them to cities far away and kept them there for four or five years, and then sent them home, while other troops replaced them.

Hangchow constantly supported a garrison of 30,000 soldiers. They were commanded by the Khan's ablest and most trusted officers, because this province, and especially its noble capital, were so wealthy and so important to him.

Marco was much interested in the nightly watch and the fire department. Mounds of earth were thrown up throughout the city, about a mile apart.

On top of each mound was a wooden frame with a sounding board. When the guard stationed there struck the board with a mallet, the sound could be heard far away. When this signal was given, the guards at the nearest bridge would seize their weapons and rush to the spot. This would occur whenever there was trouble among the people, or a fire. Fires broke out often because the houses were mostly of wood.

By the Khan's orders there was a guard of ten watchmen at every principal bridge with a shelter. Five were on duty by day and five by night. Each of these guard rooms had a metal gong and a clock. At the end of the first hour of darkness the watchmen gave a single stroke on the gongs, at the end of the second hour, two strokes, and so on through the night. Some of the watchmen patrolled the streets to see whether anyone had a light or fire burning after the hour set for putting them out. If they found anyone outdoors late at night, they arrested him, and in the morning took him to court for trial.

When a fire was discovered and the alarm

sounded, as many as one or two thousand watch-men would run from the bridges to put it out. In every street there were stone towers to which goods and furniture could be moved from houses or shops in which fires broke out. Because of the strict curfew, nobody dared to go to a fire at night, except the guards and those whose own buildings were in danger.

It happened that while Marco was in the city, the annual census was being taken. It showed that there were 1,600,000 families. Every head of a family was required to post up at the door of his house a list of everyone living there. He must also post the number of horses he owned. This was for the purpose of taxing them. When anyone died, or left the house, the name was struck out. If a child was born, it was added to the list.

Marco had marveled, when he saw so many people going and coming, how they all could be fed. But when he saw the crowded markets he understood.

In the streets connected with the market squares there were many public bathhouses, attended by both men and women. Marco was astonished to learn that everybody in the city took a cold bath every day. From childhood they had been taught that bathing in cold water was good for the health. At the public bathing places, however, there were rooms with hot water for strangers who were not used to the shock of the cold.

In other streets were the houses of the physicians and the astrologers, who also taught reading and writing and other arts. On each square were two large buildings where officers appointed by the Khan were posted, to settle any differences that might come up with the foreign merchants, or among the Chinese themselves.

While Marco was in Hangchow, he met a rich merchant who was very old. He had been a trusted member of the household of the Chinese emperor who had fled when the Mongols captured the city. He took Marco to see the ruins of the palace of the "Son of Heaven," and described to him the lavish life of the former court.

The ancestors of the emperor had built the palace on a large section of the city surrounded by high walls. The old man led Marco through a lofty gate. On each side of a flat terrace stretched a magnificent colonnade. The roofs were supported by rows of pillars, decorated beautifully in azure and gold. Opposite the entrance, at the far side of the court, was another colonnade still grander than the others. Its pillars were gilt, its roof richly adorned. The inner walls were covered with exquisite paintings showing the histories of former emperors.

Here the emperor used to hold his court and to entertain at feasts. Ten thousand persons could be seated at table under these colonnades at one time. Festivals would often last ten or twelve days. Beyond the colonnade a wall divided this outer court from the inner court of the palace. A passage led to a large cloister, its rows of pillars supporting a portico. This led to the rooms used by the emperor and his family.

From the cloister a covered corridor ran all the way down to the shore of the lake. On each side of this there were entrances to ten courts, each with fifty rooms and its own gardens. Here had lived 1,000 young women whom the king had in his service. With them and his empress he used to go down to the lake to be rowed about in barges covered with silk, and to visit temples on the shore. Nearby were quiet groves and pools, beautiful gardens full of fruit trees, and fenced-off parks for game animals, such as antelope, deer, stags and hares. Sometimes the emperor had tables loaded with foods set out in one of these groves under the shade of the lofty trees.

The Khan's viceroy now lived in the palace, and the colonnades were as splendid as ever. But since the emperor had fled, the rooms of the thousand women had been allowed to fall to ruin. Only the foundations remained. The wall that had enclosed the park and gardens was gone to decay, and there were no longer either animals or trees in them.

16

Farewell to China

As THE YEARS PASSED, Marco became more and more useful to the Khan. He was sent on secret missions "to every part of the empire," as he said proudly. Sometimes he traveled on his own, but always with the Khan's consent, and always he came back with notes on many things not known before. Because of this he was given so many honors that other men at the Khan's court became jealous of him.

His father and his uncle had not joined in his

travels. They lived near the court and became rich by trade. They began to feel a strong desire to go home to Venice, taking with them their store of gold and jewels.

The Khan was getting old. If he should die before they left, they might not have his help which they would need for the journey. They had to have the golden tablet, or royal *chop*. This would be the passport giving them free and safe conduct through every part of his dominions. They also had to have a caravan, supplies and guards.

One day, when the Khan seemed to be in better humor than usual, Nicolo Polo suddenly threw himself at his feet. He begged that he and his family be given gracious permission to go. The Khan frowned and seemed hurt. He asked why they should expose themselves to all the risks of a journey on which they might lose their lives. If wealth was what they wanted, he would give them twice what they already had. He would give them all the honors they wished. But he would not give them permission to leave because he had such high regard for them.

So they could only wait for a better chance. It came at last in a strange way.

A nephew of the Khan named Argon was King of Persia. At about this time his wife, Bolgana, died. She also had been a descendant of Genghis Khan, and her family lived at the Khan's court. As her dying wish, she asked her husband to bring to his throne no wife unless she were a member of the Mongol royal family. Anxious to carry out his wife's last request, Argon sent three ambassadors to Peking to ask that the Khan find him a wife from the same family.

By the Khan's orders a beautiful girl of seventeen, named Kogatin, was chosen and was highly approved by the ambassadors. They gathered a large caravan with many attendants, worthy to do honor to the bride of a king, and set out for Persia on a long road over deserts and mountains.

After they had traveled part of the way, they found the road blocked. War had broken out. As so often happened, the Mongol princes were fighting among themselves. One of those making trouble was probably a younger brother of Kublai

Khan himself, dreaming of taking over the empire. At any rate, the Persian ambassadors knew that they could not get through, and turned about and plodded back to the capital.

It happened that just about this time Marco came back from a sea voyage on one of his many missions for the Khan. With several ships he had been visiting the Philippine Islands and the northern coast of Indo-China. He had proved that with careful navigation it was possible to sail the southern seas. The Persian ambassadors heard this and went to talk with Marco. Between them they decided that to go home by sea would be shorter and easier than by land.

The Polos were still anxious to go. They could offer their Venetian skill in navigation, as well as Marco's recent experience among the islands. Therefore the three ambassadors, the three Polos, and with them the young princess herself, asked for an audience with the Khan.

They put all their arguments before him. At once they saw by his face that he was very displeased.

He still did not want to lose the Polos. But now they were needed by the King of Persia and his bride. If it had not been for this unusual and important chance, Marco said, they would never have been allowed to leave the Khan's service. Now at last he gave his consent.

Later he sent again for the Polos. With great kindness he asked them to promise that after they had spent some time at home with their families they would come back to him. They gave this promise. He then granted to them the royal golden *chop* as passport. He loaded them with rubies and other valuable jewels. Finally, he appointed them as his ambassadors to the Pope, the Kings of France and Spain and other Christian princes.

Down the Grand Canal again, past Yangchow where Marco had been governor, across the Yangtze River, through the familiar and gorgeous city of Hangchow for the last time, the Polos took the road to the sea. Here was well-loved country to which Marco was saying farewell, as he had said farewell to the Khan.

Towns, castles, villas, gardens, often lay so close together that it seemed as if they were riding through one long narrow city. In Fukien there were large, fierce tigers, and some savage tribes. But for most of the way they passed among cultivated people, who prospered on the manufacture of sugar, silk, cottons woven of colored threads, and fine porcelain ware, and the export of ginger and other drugs.

At Foochow they reached a broad river lined on both banks with large buildings. Lying alongside were ships that had come up river from the sea, ships from India with pearls and jewels to exchange for the sugar and other products of China.

Crossing the river, they came down to the harbor of Zayton, near Amoy. This was one of the greatest ports in the world. Ships came here from everywhere, carrying all kinds of goods. The long and greedy arm of the Khan reached out to take a heavy tax on every shipload.

But along this southward road Marco had once again found the Chinese people well-to-do, peaceable and fond of ease. "The country is delightful," he said in final comment at this port where he was leaving China—never to return, although he could not yet know that.

17

The Voyage

IN THE HARBOR stood the fleet of ships that the
Polos were to navigate to the Persian Gulf. There
were fourteen vessels, each with four masts and
nine sails. Four or five were large enough to carry
crews of 250 men. Below deck they had as many
as sixty separate cabins. The holds of the larger
ships were divided by bulkheads of thick planks.
This was because they might spring a leak by strik-
ing a rock or a whale. Marco gravely said that often a hungry whale, attracted by the white foam

of a moving ship, would rush at it expecting something to eat and would hit the ship and crack the bottom. When this happened the cargo could be moved and that part of the hold repaired, without flooding the other tightly fitted bulkheads. Thus Marco told six centuries ago of a way of ship-building which is used, on a greater scale, in modern warships and liners.

The Princess and the Persian ambassadors had reached the port. With the Polos they went on board. One by one the ships hoisted their sails and moved out of the harbor.

There were about two thousand men and women in the expedition. By order of the Khan they carried stores and provisions enough for two years. The voyage took almost that long.

Steering to the southwest, they made for the Gulf of Tonkin, inside Hainan Island. The gulf was so large, and there were so many people on its many islands, that Marco exclaimed, "It seems like another world!" After sailing for two months he made a landing on the coast of Indo-China. Here was a kingdom which the Khan had conquered some years before. It now sent to him each year as tribute great loads of sweet-scented wood to be used for incense, and twenty of its largest and handsomest elephants.

This was the last point at which Marco felt the full power of the Khan. His next landing, hundreds of miles to the south, was on the Malay Peninsula which was, as he said, "governed by its own king, who pays no tribute to any other."

Sailing on past Singapore, Marco noticed that he was so far south that he could no longer see the north star. He was very near the equator. Then the ships veered northwest through the Straits of Malacca. They had run as far as the northern tip of Sumatra when the winds turned against them. The famous and terrible monsoon, which struck each year, had begun. They could only wait until it was over. They anchored and went ashore.

The people of the country were savages, and Marco had heard that they were cannibals. Being in charge of the expedition, he at once had a deep trench dug on the land side, with its ends coming down to the harbor where the ships lay.

He had logs cut and several blockhouses built
along the trench. Within this fortification they
lived in safety for five whole months while the
monsoon blew.

They traded for food and other things with the
natives, who gradually grew friendly. As usual,
Marco went out among them and learned much
about their customs. They made bread from the
pith of a tree called *sago*. Eating the bread, he
found that it tasted like barley, and he put some

sago away to take home to Venice. He also took home the seeds of a plant from which they made a fine dye, but later he found that it would not grow in the warm climate of Italy.

There were cocoanuts that grew to the size of a man's head, and he thought their milk was better flavored than any other drink he had ever had. He was much impressed by the one-horned rhinoceroses, which "take delight in muddy pools, and are filthy in their habits."

At last, in September, the monsoon ended. The wind was favorable again and the fleet set sail.

After crossing the wide Bay of Bengal, they landed on the island of Ceylon. Here, although the island had its own king, Marco learned how far Kublai Khan had reached out to try to take what he wanted. He heard two stories about that.

Ceylon was rich in precious stones—sapphires, topazes, amethysts, garnets, and above all, rubies that were the most beautiful and valuable in the world. The king of Ceylon owned a ruby as thick as a man's arm, without a single flaw. It looked like a glowing fire. The fame of this stone was so great that it had reached the ears of the Khan in distant Peking. He sent ambassadors to buy it for him and offered as his price "the value of a whole city." But the king of Ceylon had replied proudly that the jewel had been handed down to him by the kings who had sat on the throne before him, and that he would not sell it "for all the treasure in the universe."

The Khan had better luck with his second demand. In this island there is a high mountain, rocky and steep and very hard to climb. It was called Adam's Peak, because there was a legend that on the very top was the tomb of Adam, the first man. This legend was denied by Buddhists, who said that the tomb was that of Buddha, the founder of their religion. They believed, wrongly, that Buddha had been the son of a king of Ceylon. The son had refused to accept any worldly goods and had fled to the top of the mountain to live a religious life alone and in poverty. When he died, the grief-stricken father had an image of his son made of gold and precious stones. He ordered every person on the island to worship it as a god.

This, Marco was told, was the origin of the worship of idols there. Pilgrims in great numbers came from far and near to climb the mountain and see the relics which the priests showed them —some of Buddha's hair, his teeth and a basin he had used. Arab pilgrims came too, but they insisted that the relics had belonged to Adam, their own prophet.

Some of these Arabs had traveled on to China, and had told Kublai Khan what they had seen. In his usual way the Khan decided that he must own those relics. He sent ambassadors to get them from the king of Ceylon. This time they were successful. They came back with two large back teeth, some of the hair and a handsome basin made of porphyry. When the Khan heard that the returning ambassadors were near the capital, he was so excited that he ordered all the people of the city to go out to meet them, and they were escorted to the throne room "with great pomp and solemnity." This final tale was the climax of Marco's long record of the greatness of Kublai Khan.

Taking ship again, he sailed westward sixty miles to the southern shores of India. This, he soon decided, was "the noblest and richest country in the world."

18

India

MARCO and his expedition spent several months in southern India, going from harbor to harbor. Again he was making notes of people and customs that were strange to him.

First he studied the pearl fishing in a bay on the Coromandel Coast. Many boats of different sizes were anchored in the shallow bay. He watched the skilled divers plunge to the bottom with bags of netting fastened to their waists. They would stay down, gathering the pearl oysters, as long as they could hold their breath. Coming to the surface, they would rest a little, then dive again. This they could keep up all day long.

It was not a safe job, for the water was full of man-eating sharks. So the owners of the boats took along with them magicians known as "shark charmers." These men were supposed to have the power of enchanting all kinds of beasts and birds, and could stupefy the sharks and prevent them from attacking the divers. When the day's fishing ended, the charm was taken off so that anyone who tried to steal oysters at night would be driven away by the sharks. For their services the shark charmers were given one-twentieth of the value of the pearls found.

As his right the king of the region received one-tenth of the pearls. He was also given first choice of the finest, which he bought for good prices. The king, like the rest of his people, wore almost no clothing. But he had always around his neck a rosary of 104 pearls and rubies. For his religion required that he repeat a prayer so many times a day, and the prayer was the word for "Lord" repeated one hundred and four times, which he counted off on the pearls and jewels as if they were beads.

On each arm and leg the king wore three jeweled gold bracelets, and on his toes as well as on his fingers were valuable rings. He could afford this, Marco remarked, because all the pearls and jewels were products of his own dominion.

When a king died his son took the throne, but did not inherit the treasure. He was expected to gather as much as his father had. In this way, Marco supposed, immense wealth was stored up generation after generation. Once more he had a story to take home that would excite the greed of future explorers.

He did not approve of all the ways of the Indians. Because he did not understand some of them, such as marriage customs, he gave some unfair impressions. But much of what he told was true.

He told of the evil tradition that when a man died and his body was burned, his wife must throw her body on the funeral pyre and be burned with him. He told of the worship of cattle.

In China he had been surprised by daily bathing, but here he found that both men and women washed their whole bodies in water *twice* every day. In the morning they would neither eat nor drink until after they had bathed, and then there would be another bath in the evening. Anyone who did not do this was disgraced. In eating they used only the right hand, and they never touched their food with the left hand, which was used for all unclean purposes. Every person had his own drinking cup and never drank out of that of anyone else. They never put the cup to their lips, but held it above them and poured the drink into the mouth.

Marco thought highly of the Indians' strict sense of justice. If a man kept putting off the payment of a debt, his creditor would draw a circle around him. If the debtor should try to step out of the circle, he would be liable to punishment by death. Marco himself saw an example of this. For a long time the king had owed money to a foreign merchant. One day when he was riding horseback the merchant came out of the crowd and drew a circle around the king and his horse. The king stopped at once and did not move out of the circle until the debt was paid in full. The bystanders who saw this exclaimed that the king deserved the title of "Most Just" because he himself obeyed the law.

The Indians judged the hour of the day by the length of a man's shadow when he was standing erect. Every day of the week there was one hour

which they called unlucky, and on these hours they would not do any kind of business, because they thought it would not be successful. They had books which listed the qualities of every day in the entire year. When a baby was born, the father or mother at once wrote down the very hour of the birth as well as the day of the month, and also, as Marco put it, "the age of the moon." This was because every future act of the baby's life would be regulated by astrology.

Marco thought very well of the character of Indian merchants—"the best and most honorable that can be found," he said. They would never tell a lie, even though their lives might depend upon it. They hated theft. When a foreign merchant, not knowing the customs of the country, asked an Indian merchant to take care of his business for him, he could be sure it would be done well and honestly. The Indian would not accept any payment for his services.

These merchants had their superstitions. When one was about to buy something, he would look at his own shadow cast in the sunshine. If it was not as large as it should be, he would not buy anything that day. When he was going out of his house, if he heard anyone sneeze, he would go right back into the house and stay at home.

Marco wrote respectfully about the Indian holy men, who were called *yogi*. "They do not deprive any creature of life, not even a fly, a flea, or a louse, because they believe they have souls, and

to feed upon any animal they consider a great sin. They do not even eat vegetables or roots until they have become dry, because they think that these also have souls. They make no use of spoons or plates, but spread their food upon leaves. They live to a great age, some of them even to a hundred and fifty years, enjoying health and vigor although they sleep upon the bare earth."

The Indian habit of chewing betel nut and spitting out the red juice seemed to Marco disgusting, but he was told that it was good for the health.

The fabulous wealth of India was not only in jewels. There were precious spices, the hides of many animals, the finest cottons in the world, and beautifully manufactured goods such as bed coverlets of red and blue leather, very soft and stitched with gold and silver thread, cushions ornamented with gold wire in the form of birds and beasts, and the most delicate embroideries that Marco had ever seen.

Trading ships came from China and the West to bring these and many other goods to the seaports. As Marco moved northward along the Indian coast, he began to see vessels from Arabia and the Persian Gulf toward which he was bound. He saw ahead the end of his long voyage.

When he rounded the southern tip of India, at Cape Cormorin, he made a note that he had seen a part of the northern constellation, which he had missed in Sumatra. He tried to guess how high above the horizon it appeared to be. A little farther up the coast he noted that the north star is seen "about two fathoms above the horizon." And again, some time later, "Here the north star is seen still higher." He was thinking eagerly of home.

19

Homeward

AT EVERY port Marco met traders and sailors from everywhere. He was not only a good observer; he also was a good listener. He wrote down what they told him about places he did not visit himself. It must be admitted that in this way he got the false as well as the true. You find in his book tales that are also in the *Arabian Nights*, such as the voyages of Sinbad the Sailor.

He heard of the "islands of males and females," where all the men lived on one island and all the women on the other, except for the three spring months when the men came to visit and sow the grain which the women had to harvest in the autumn.

He heard about Socotra, where the people used much witchcraft. They knew how to put a spell on a pirate so that the wind would wreck his ship, or becalm him, or blow him right back to their island where they could make him pay for the damage he had done.

Marco listened with wonder to the account of the roc, the bird so large and strong that it could pick up an elephant with its talons. He was told that Kublai Khan had sent messengers to inquire about this and they had brought back a huge feather.

In Zanzibar, they said, were very tall men who could carry loads that would call for four Venetians—but they needed as much food as five! Giraffes were described to him, and "monkeys that have the figures of men." He learned about the Nile River. Ships from India with spices and drugs unloaded at the Arabian port of Aden. Their cargoes were put on smaller vessels and sent up the Red Sea to a point where they were loaded on the backs of camels. For thirty days the camels plodded overland until they reached the Nile, where again the goods were put on small vessels and taken to Cairo and Alexandria. It seemed like a clumsy route, but Marco saw that it was after all the shortest and easiest from India to Egypt. Back to India, from Aden and other ports, went shiploads of fine Arabian horses.

But Marco and his ships did not sail along the Arabian coast. They swung into the Gulf of Oman and landed on the island of Hormuz. This was where the Polos, long ago, had meant to sail for China. But the ships had looked to them unsafe, and they had turned back to take the long overland trail. This, too, was where the heat had been so terrible. Now there had been an air-conditioning improvement, or possibly Marco had not noticed it before. Every house had ventilators which sent air into every room on every floor as it was wanted. "Without this," said Marco, "it would be impossible to live in the place."

Ships with spices from India unloaded at the port.

The sea voyage was over. Of the 2,000 men and women who had started from China two years ago, 600 men had died. Only one of the three Persian ambassadors had survived. But all but one of the many women, including the Princess and her many attendants, had lived to reach Persia safely.

They left the ships. Ahead lay the caravan journey into Persia where they must deliver the Princess.

No sooner was Marco ashore than he was told that King Argon was dead. It was to him that they were to bring the Princess, to be his bride. What should they now do with her?

Argon's son Kasan would succeed him, but Kasan was still very young. His uncle Kiakatu had taken control of the country, to hold it for almost five years until the Prince should be of age. The Polos asked the uncle for instructions. He told them to take the Princess to the young prince. Kasan was then in camp on the eastern border of Persia near the great salt desert. He was with an army of 60,000 men guarding an important pass between two mountains against a threatened invasion.

The Polos with the Princess set out over the familiar road which they had traveled on their first journey many years ago. It led through Persia to the edge of the desert. Here they found the Prince. He was not as tall or as handsome as his father Argon had been. But he was young, and he was of the family of Kublai Khan. The Princess was soon married to him.

The duty of the three Polos was done. Kiakatu, as the temporary ruler of the country, gave them four large golden tablets on which were inscribed orders for their safe conduct. The inscription said that the name of Kublai Khan must be held in reverence and that the three Polos as his ambassadors must be treated with honor. All their expenses must be paid, and they must be given escort. In many places they were escorted by as many as two hundred horsemen. These were needed as they traveled northward, because the rule of Kiakatu was unpopular. The people of Persia were likely to "commit insults and outrage," said Marco, as they would not have done under their proper king.

Soon came shocking news. Kublai Khan was dead of old age, at seventy-nine. The Polos had promised him that they would return. Now they need never go again. Death had released them from their pledge.

They pressed on to the shore of the Black Sea, at Trebizond. There they found passage on a ship westward to Constantinople, through the straits, to Negropont, and finally home to Venice, "safely arrived in the year 1295."

20

Venice and Genoa

THIS WAS the end of the story as Marco himself told it.

Many years later another man, named Ramusio, told about the Polos' return to Venice. Off the ship, they came to their old home in coarse and shabby clothes. They had "a smack of the Mongol in both manner and accent." No one recognized them, not even their own relatives. But when they invited all their kin to a feast, all came. Marco and his father and his uncle appeared at the dinner table in handsome robes of red satin. Between courses they went out and changed to other robes of red damask, and then again to red velvet. Their astonished guests did not know that this changing of costumes was a custom they had learned at the court of Kublai Khan.

At the end of the dinner Marco went into the next room. He came out carrying the shabby garments in which they had arrived in Venice. Taking sharp knives, the three Polos ripped open the seams of the clothing. Out fell a stream of jewels —diamonds, rubies, emeralds, sapphires. Marco heaped them on the tables as their guests gaped. This was his home-coming triumph.

The whole city of Venice heard the news. Marco was greeted everywhere with honors. He began to tell the stories of his adventures and discoveries. He spoke especially of what he had seen at the court of Kublai Khan. It seemed that he was always talking of millions—"millions of this" and "millions of that." And so it was that he got his nickname, Marco Millions.